Slave State

Other Books of Interest from St. Augustine's Press

Slave State
A New Reading of George Orwell's
1984

DAVID LOWENTHAL

How the Quest for a Perfect Society Led Instead to the
Worst—in the Course of Revolting against Which the True
Ends of Life Are Established

ST. AUGUSTINE'S PRESS
South Bend, Indiana

Manufactured in the United States of America.

1 2 3 4 5 6   26 25 24 23 22 21

Library of Congress Control Number: 2021944293

paperback ISBN: 978-1-58731-843-6
epub ISBN 978-1-58731-844-3

∞ The paper used in this publication meets the minimum requirements of the American National Standard for Information Sciences – Permanence of Paper for Printed Materials, ANSI Z39.48-1984.

St. Augustine's Press
www.staugustine.net

CONTENTS

Introduction

I first learned of George Orwell through the letters he wrote from London for *The Partisan Review* during World War II. I loved him then and I love him still. Whatever he did had the touch of an independent mind and a noble soul. Nobody could write more clearly. Nobody felt more deeply and sincerely for the underdog. Nobody had as much to say about the problems pressing humanity. No one did more to appreciate the achievements of modernity while facing its grim realities. Nobody made a greater effort to rise above the petty orthodoxies of the left toward a better general appreciation of liberal society and his own England. None of the literary people gave nearly as much independent thought to the standards that should guide human life and must guide it in the dark days ahead.

1984 was published in 1949, shortly after Orwell's death. For decades it was considered the classic portrayal of communist totalitarianism and taught in the schools as such. After the collapse of the Soviet Union its popularity waned—not even to be revived by Solzhenitsyn's description of the horrors of Soviet Communism. Solzhenitsyn wrote as a Russian patriot and a Christian, Orwell as a democratic socialist who shared the vision of Western liberal enlightenment and was perplexed, as much as he was appalled, by the growth of totalitarianism and the totalitarian mentality in the twentieth century. We can see why communism absorbed his thought much more than

Nazism or fascism. While all three had much in common, communism claimed to be the final extension of reason in the name of liberty and equality—i.e., in the name of human brotherhood rather than drastic inequality. How, at the very moment when science and technology promised the final liberation of mankind, could communism turn mankind toward its universal, complete, and perpetual enslavement, culminating in an earthly hell rather than an earthly paradise?

1984 is an attempt to answer this question. But, beyond this, and at least equally important, it is an attempt to guide mankind in the dark days ahead—the dark ages ahead—which, in the aftermath of atomic war, Orwell considered not simply possible but most likely. There is no positive political message in *1984*: the closest to it comes in the appendix on Newspeak, where the second paragraph of the Declaration of Independence ("We hold these truths to be self-evident, etc.") is used to demonstrate language from the pre-revolutionary world that cannot be translated into Newspeak. But there is a positive moral message—one often missed by commentators because, unlike Goldstein's extensive treatise on oligarchical collectivism, it is woven into the fabric of the novel as a whole—into its characters, their words, their actions. Through the movement of the novel, Orwell tries to impress on the passions, hearts, and minds of his readers the most valuable lessons concerning the right and wrong way to live. With the decline of Christianity's influence in forming the moral sense of the West and the concomitant increase in power hunger, wielding instruments born of modern enlightenment, what mankind most needed was moral guidance, conveyed not abstractly, through philosophy, but in such a way as to grip the whole soul.

This moral teaching, this "humanist ethic," as Orwell calls it elsewhere, was his greatest bequest to mankind. It sought to care for intellectuals and masses alike, for the heroic and the common, for the aristocratic "Winston" and the democratic "Smith"—as the name of his protagonist itself suggests. Based on the study of human nature and the discovery of man's good in his nature, it tries to convey a palpable knowledge of good and evil and thus to assure the passing on of the human heritage from hand to hand or mouth to mouth should the threatening blackness engulf us. Understanding this teaching along with the deeper causes of the tyranny is the prime objects of this study, consequent to which—apart from a brief opening sketch—only minimal attention will be given to the details of Orwell's life or to those many writings that do not bear directly on our subject.

Orwell was a literary man of the left, an intellectual but not an ordinary one. He suffered from the rupture between literature and philosophy that afflicts both to this day and, while few knew modern literature better, he had little taste for the abstractions of philosophy and knew little of the ancient or modern political philosophers who could have helped him most. Yet his thinking points toward philosophy, needs it for its beginnings, development, and completion. Properly understood it can even serve as a bridge to philosophy, and that's how I regard it here. But first we must be sure we see the real Orwell, the full Orwell, and that requires some doing. He was a much more systematic thinker than he is given credit for—an adverse opinion easily come by since he wrote so many different things without ever systematically summing up his thought. I have tried to examine these writings under relevant heads to ascertain his moral and political views by the time he wrote *1984*. And because there's no substitute for his own words, I have cited passages copiously, often from writings the reader might find it difficult to obtain for himself. As we witness the intellectual process by which Orwell ultimately abandons the Marxism with which he began, we come upon countless themes and issues of great currency today on which I shall not myself dwell, leaving it to the thoughtful reader to consider these ties to the contemporary. My own comments will occur briefly from time to time and are mostly suggestive in nature.

Lest we be tempted to dismiss Orwell's account of the totalitarian regime in *1984* as of merely historical interest, let us ask ourselves whether the conditions lending support to that regime have completely disappeared. First, regarding the work's premise of nuclear war, has that possibility declined or increased with the current and prospective proliferation of nuclear might? Do we know what human life would be like in its aftermath? Have we not already discovered means of wreaking havoc even worse than the atom bomb itself? Is not Communist China consciously preparing to overtake, overcome, and perhaps overthrow our liberal society? At the same time, a much greater centralization of power has occurred here. As for devices watching and controlling us, we have already gone beyond the capacities used so coercively in *1984*. Nor can we really think the totalitarian mentality a thing of the past, with so much evidence to the contrary regularly displayed in so many ways—on college campuses, at rock concerts, in ordinary political life. The massing of people in cities and the grip of modern industry, the spread of drugs, and wealth itself have taken their toll and left us more prone to the siren calls of false heroism. There's much more crowd behavior, much less independent thought. The sense of personal worth, virtue, and privacy itself has been eroded by the mass media. With the decline of religious beliefs and feelings and out of narrow self-interest many have even come to welcome late-term abortions. With the help of technical advances the sexual impulse, already widely emancipated and promoted by the purveyors of intellect as they battered down the walls of religion, wreaked havoc on the family and left rootless individuals in their place. Many of the educated, influenced by relativism in its many forms, have lost confidence in the liberal principles that in the world of *1984* have been completely effaced. This is especially true on college campuses, where faculty, administration, and students collaborate in fostering a radical contempt for their own country. At the same time we have abandoned inculcating good citizenship, higher ideals, and a sense of personal worth in the schools, encouraging instead an aimless low-level conformist "individuality" just waiting to be harnessed together and directed. Given these conditions, can we be sure we have left the conditions leading to the horrors of *1984* far behind as mere fiction?

Part One
Orwell's Moral and Political Standards before *1984*

Sketch of His Life and Writings

Orwell's thought and action were bound up with the rights and wrongs, promises and menaces, of secular machine civilization. Born in 1903 and educated at the renowned Eton, he was, according to his own account, both a snob and a revolutionary by the age of seventeen. Following graduation he became a British policeman in Burma (1922–27) and there developed an "immense sense of guilt" for having assisted in the oppression of the natives. On returning to Europe, and by way of expiation, he spent more than a year in self-inflicted hoboism, sharing the life of the downtrodden and afterwards recording his experiences in *Down and Out in Paris and London* (1933). During the great Depression he managed to eke out a living by one means or another and at the same time produced his first three novels: *Burmese Days* (1933), *The Clergyman's Daughter* (1935), and *Keep the Aspidistra Flying* (1936). In 1936 he spent several months living with another group of the poor—this time British coal miners. By then he had become a confirmed though unorthodox socialist, for whom ideology was much less important than real concern for the people, and in *The Road to Wigan Pier* (1937) he made public both his first-hand observations showing the need for socialism and his critique of the contemporary socialist movement. In 1937 he fought on the Republican side in Spain until wounded, learning directly of the Communist threat to freedom and recounting his experiences in *Homage to Catalonia* (1938). The next year, in *Coming Up For Air*, his last novel prior to *1984*, he portrayed lower middle-class English life in the shadow of totalitarianism and a second World War. During the early years of the war, especially in *The Lion and the Unicorn* (1941), he wrote to encourage a socialist revolution in England as the only means by which Hitler could be repulsed and defeated. Here his hopes for an overall social change in England reached their peak, only to fade as he became more pessimistic regarding revolutions and the future of mankind. He saw no fundamental changes forthcoming from the new Labor government and feared that the atom bomb and the growth in power of Soviet Russia made another and greater war likely soon. Although he had been busy during the war with essays and articles that had already won him a following, Orwell's name did not receive wide prominence until the publication of *Animal Farm* in 1945. With its stark simplicity, this allegorical satire of communist revolution became a popular classic overnight. Two years later Orwell retired to the island of Jura in the Hebrides and worked on *1984*, barely completing it before the tuberculosis with which he had long been afflicted took his life in January 1950.

Critique of Perfectionism

Let's begin by gathering together the central moral and political themes of Orwell's thought prior to *1984*, relying primarily on his essays. Humanism, the philosophy he avowed, was in his mind distinguished not only from the supernaturalism of religion but also from those non-religious doctrines and ways of life that either espouse a similar perfectionism or are in other ways inconsiderate of the full complement of man's natural needs. Humanism's main concern is man's happiness, and the question of the possibility of making happiness a normal human condition constitutes the crux of serious political controversy.

In his essays on Tolstoy (1947) and Gandhi (1948)—outstanding modern figures in different religious traditions—Orwell presents his objections to what might be generalized as the ideal of saintliness. Like most modern intellectuals, he takes it for granted that religion is essentially wishful myth-making and concentrates on the good or bad effects of religious belief. This procedure implies the existence of knowable norms of good and evil independent of religion and its God. What are these, and how are they known?

According to Orwell, Shakespeare's later tragedies are exemplars of the humanist point of view. These plays "...start out with the humanist assumption that life, although full of sorrow, is worth living, and that Man is a noble animal...."[1] Tolstoy's saintly ideal, on the other hand, constitutes an abandonment of human life in favor of a life to come:

> If only, Tolstoy says in effect, we would stop breeding, fighting, struggling and enjoying, if we could get rid not only of our sins but of everything else that binds us to the surface of the earth—including love, then the whole painful process would be over

and the Kingdom of Heaven would arrive.… Ultimately it is the Christian attitude which is self-in-
terested and hedonistic, since the aim is always to
get away from the painful struggle of earthly life
and find eternal peace in some kind of Heaven or
Nirvana.[2]

The saint is one who spiritualizes himself—i.e., cripples his
natural faculties—in the hope of future reward, and his convictions may even encourage the use of worldly coercion in one
form or another as a means of bringing others into the service
of his ideal.

Gandhi is more admirable—"…an interesting and unusual
man who enriched the world simply by being alive." But his
teachings "…cannot be squared with the belief that Man is the
measure of all things, and that our job is to make life worth
living on this earth, which is the only earth we have." His
saintly ideal enjoins the avoidance of animal foods, alcohol, tobacco, spices, sexual intercourse and even sexual desire, and finally all close friendships and exclusive loves. Here is what
Orwell says in reply:

The essence of being human is that one does not
seek perfection, that one is sometimes willing to
commit sins for the sake of loyalty, that one does
not push asceticism to the point where it makes
friendly intercourse impossible, and that one is prepared in the end to be defeated and broken up by
life, which is the inevitable price of fastening one's
love upon other human individuals. No doubt

alcohol, tobacco, and so forth, are things a saint
must avoid, but sainthood is also a thing human beings must avoid.[3]

Hence, while Orwell admires Gandhi's personal courage,
truthfulness and loftiness, he insists nevertheless that one must
be for Man and his earthly existence rather than for God and
other-worldliness.

   In these passages Orwell opposes both the hedonism that
calculates the worth of actions by the sum of pleasure conveyed
to the actor and the perfectionism that seeks to reduce to a
minimum man's natural attachment to earthly things. His humanism locates the good in the preservation of the whole of
man's nature without retreating in the face of sufferings that
will have to be endured. No part of man's nature is evil, and the
right course of action is to keep doing the human things for
their own sake, accepting the unhappiness that thus forms an
essential ingredient of human life. The human is shed by the
saint in favor of the divine, by the hedonist in favor of his ego,
but psychologically the two have in common a desire to escape
from the pain and hard work involved in a natural life.

   In his essay on *Gulliver's Travels* (1946), Orwell objects to
Swift's having claimed for Reason what Tolstoy and Gandhi
later claimed for spirituality:

Happiness is notoriously difficult to describe, and
pictures of a just and well-ordered Society are sel-
dom either attractive or convincing. Most creators
of "favorable" Utopias, however, are concerned to
show what life could be like if it were lived more

fully. Swift advocates a simple refusal of life, justifying this by the claim that "Reason" consists in thwarting your instincts. The Houyhnhnms, creatures without a history, continue for generation after generation to live prudently, maintaining their population at exactly the same level, avoiding all passion, suffering from no diseases, meeting death indifferently, training up their young in the same principles—and all for what? In order that the same process may continue indefinitely. The notions that life here and now is worth living, or that it must be sacrificed for some future good, are all absent. The dreary world of the Houyhnhnms was about as good a Utopia as Swift could construct, granting that he neither believed in a "next world" nor could get any pleasure out of certain normal activities. But it is not really set up as something desirable in itself, but as the justification for another attack on humanity. The aim, as usual, is to humiliate Man by reminding him that he stinks; and the ultimate motive, probably, is a kind of envy, the envy of the ghost for the living, of the man who knows he cannot be happy for the others who—so he fears—may be a little happier than himself.[4]

Again it is the thwarting of the natural instincts with their accompanying joys and sorrows, whether in the name of spiritual or rational perfection, that Orwell rejects. Orwell also claims that Swift opposes science practiced freely for its own sake, as well as advancing technology, individual liberty, and democracy.

Swift's ideal is "…a static, incurious civilization," a totalitarian society "…where there can be no freedom and no development." Swift is against social progress in the modern sense; in short, he denies that man as we normally find him is a noble animal, and that life is worth living and can be made more so.

Although Orwell sees clearly that Swift is an admirer of classical pagan reason and virtue rather than Christian spirituality, he fails to associate him and his utopia with the philosophies of Plato and Aristotle. Nevertheless, one can say that through Swift Orwell rejects the classical view of human perfection, and on such typically modern grounds as the claims of the instincts, individuality, inventiveness, and social progress. But he views neither the spiritual nor the rational perfectionists with sufficient sympathy or interest. He rejects both hedonism and perfectionism because they are false to human nature and lead, in their application, to vast social harm. But how will humanism preserve the whole of human nature without discovering some way of resolving the conflicts posed by its parts, or without maintaining that some of its parts are worthier or higher than others? In particular, can reason and the passions have equal status and dignity in the human soul? What did he mean by calling man a noble animal?

Critique of Hedonism

In Orwell's usage, hedonism is of two sorts, the one selfish, the other altruistic. Either can tend toward the vulgar by stressing the primacy of bodily pleasures, but the altruistic kind derives from a moral dedication to the good of mankind; it aims at using scientific technology to liberate human life from scarcity and suffering and to help men live together as free and equal brothers. The term "hedonistic" applies with special emphasis to those who consider this social ideal not only desirable but eminently practicable.

While strongly rejecting selfish hedonism, Orwell's attitude toward what might be called the social-scientific variety is a mixed one—both with respect to its desirability and its practicability. His ambivalence on the count of desirability is most manifest in *The Road to Wigan Pier's* criticism of H. G. Wells and the Marxists. To both he attributes the view that a society based on the fullest development of science and technology is best equipped to suit man's needs and to make possible the solution of his most important problems. The twelfth chapter of *Road* contains Orwell's summary of the "intelligent" and "sensitive" man's objections to unending progress in technology. By guaranteeing man against a host of difficulties, the machine lessens his need for physical, intellectual, and moral exertion and prowess. The "comely attributes" necessary to being fully human will slowly disappear, leaving a race of little, fat, soft men to enjoy their artificial world of order and efficiency. In other words, the more admirable kind of hedonism reduces to the vulgar sort by virtue of its very success. But human life requires work and effort and the exercise of the various natural capacities: "For man is not, as the vulgarer hedonists seem to suppose, a kind of walking stomach; he has also got a hand, an eye and a brain." The thought that H. G. Wells dares not face is:

> ...that the machine itself may be the enemy. So in
> his more characteristic Utopias *(The Dream, Men*

Like Gods, etc.) he returns to optimism and a vision
of enlightened sunbathers whose sole topic of con-
versation is their own superiority to their ancestors.
Brave New World belongs to a later time and to a
generation which has seen through the swindle of
"progress."[5]

This criticism is as mordant as it is funny. Unfortunately,
Orwell admits, the impulse to invent and improve typical of
recent Western civilization has itself become a machine, and
suggestions that it be checked or controlled are regarded on all
sides as blasphemous. On occasion (as we have just seen) he
even expresses antagonism to machine or industrial civilization
as such. But what is the alternative?

When one pictures a desirable civilization, one pictures it merely as an objective; there is no need to
pretend that it has ever existed in space or time.
Press this point home, explain that you wish merely
to make life simpler and harder instead of softer and
more complex, and the Socialist will usually assume
that you want to revert to a "state of nature"—
meaning some stinking Paleolithic cave: as though
there were nothing between a flint scraper and the
steel mills of Sheffield, or between a skin coracle
and the Queen Mary.[6]

Is there no middle ground? Something similar is said even
more clearly in that part of his essay on Henry Miller (1940)
dealing with English writers who repudiated modernity:

"When Lawrence prefers the Etruscans (his Etruscans) to ourselves it is difficult not to agree with him, and yet, after all, it is a species of defeatism, because that is not the direction in which the world is moving." Since the machine is here to stay, only socialism is capable of employing it to further justice and liberty for the whole people. But it must be a humanized socialism, in which the machine is eyed suspiciously as something in the nature of a drug. To form a permanent humanizing opposition within the socialist movement is the proper task of intelligent and sensitive people today.

Orwell fears that social-scientific hedonism will lose sight of the "comely attributes" and the full man but his sympathy for the common man prevents him from accepting the scarcity, brute labor, inequality, and oppression characteristic (as he thought) of pre-scientific or pre-modern life, thus in some degree likening it to the "state of nature" and in fact leaving man with two basic possibilities—the pre-modern and the modern. He frequently insists that the needs of the body are more urgent, though not higher, than the needs of the soul: "A human being is primarily a bag for putting food into; the other functions and faculties may be more godlike, but in point of time they come afterwards." Or again, in a later essay on the Spanish civil war (1943):

All that the working man demands is what these others would consider the indispensable minimum without which human life could not be lived at all. Enough to eat, freedom from the haunting fear of unemployment, the knowledge that your children will get a fair chance, a bath once a day, clean linen reasonably often, a roof that doesn't leak, and short enough working hours to leave you with a little energy when the day is done. Not one of those who preach against "materialism" would consider life livable without these things. And how easily that minimum could be attained if we chose to set our minds to it for only twenty years! To raise the standard of living of the whole world to that of Britain would not be a greater undertaking than the war we have just fought. I don't claim, and I don't know who does, that that would solve anything in itself. It is merely that privation and brute labor have to be abolished before the real problems of humanity can be tackled. The major problem of our time is the decay of the belief in personal immortality, and it cannot be dealt with while the average human being is either drudging like an ox or shivering in fear of the secret police. How right the working classes are in their "materialism"! How right they are to realize that the belly comes before the soul, not in the scale of values but in point of time! Understand that and the long horror that we are enduring becomes at least intelligible.[7]

Orwell's dilemma is now manifest: care for the bodily wants of all men comes first, care for their higher needs later, but bodily wants set into motion an age of science and technology that tends to worship the body and discard the soul, ending in vulgar hedonism. He recognizes that the decay in the belief in personal immortality is the major problem, but he is confident that even without God and personal immortality, men can find their bearings and develop a conception of the most worthy life by which to guide, and give meaning to, their actions. He also realizes that setting bounds to the machine, and to hedonism, is extremely unpopular with capitalists and socialists alike. In fact, even his own writings waver on the amount of machine technology and the level of abundance that should characterize a socialist society.

In one of Orwell's newspaper columns from the year 1944 there is further evidence of the seriousness with which he considered the problem of replacing the Christian ethic and scheme of meaning:

> Western civilization, unlike some Oriental civilizations, was founded partly on the belief in individual immortality. If one looks at the Christian religion from the outside, this belief appears far more important than the belief in God. The Western conception of good and evil is very difficult to separate from it. There is little doubt that the modern cult of power worship is bound up with modern man's feelings that life here and now is the only life there is. If death ends everything, it becomes much harder to believe that you can be in the right if you are defeated. Statesmen, nations, theories, causes are judged almost inevitably by the test of material success. Supposing that one can separate the two phenomena, I would say that the decay of the belief in personal immortality has been as important as the rise of machine civilization. Machine civilization has terrible possibilities, as you probably reflected

the other night when the ack-ack guns started up:
but the other thing has terrible possibilities too, and
it cannot be said that the Socialist movement has
given much thought to them.

I do not want the belief in life after death to return, and in any case it is not likely to return. What
I do point out is that its disappearance has left a big
hole, and that we ought to take notice of that fact.
Reared for thousands of years on the notion that
the individual survives, man has got to make a considerable psychological effort to get used to the notion that the individual perishes. He is not likely to
salvage civilization unless he can evolve a system of
good and evil which is independent of heaven and
hell. Marxism, indeed, does supply this, but it has
never really been popularized. Most Socialists are
content to point out that once Socialism has been
established we shall be happier in a material sense,
and to assume that all problems lapse when one's
belly is full. But the truth is the opposite: when
one's belly is empty, one's only problem is an empty
belly. It is when we have got away from drudgery
and exploitation that we shall really start wondering
about man's destiny and the reason for his existence.
One cannot have any worthwhile picture of the future unless one realizes how much we have lost by
the decay of Christianity.[8]

Orwell sees much more deeply than the socialists generally and
Marx himself. The loss of the belief in personal immortality is

an enormous problem for mankind. To salvage civilization, the greatest need is for "a system of good and evil which is independent of heaven and hell." And he insists that a socialist civilization without such a system will hardly be worthwhile. Nevertheless, he seems hopeful that his socialist colleagues can be convinced of the need for adopting something superior to their hedonism, and this something is said to have its basis in Marxism itself—a very questionable claim.

In another newspaper article almost two years later (1946), Orwell focuses his attention on the "modern civilized man's idea of pleasure" and in so doing sums up what he means by the humanist ethic. Having read of an imaginary ultra-modern "pleasure spot," providing, within a large scientifically constructed and controlled area all the recreation and amusement that a "tired and life-hungry man" could want, he proceeds to compare its underlying ideas with those of Coleridge's "Kublai Khan":

> When one looks at Coleridge's very different conception of a "pleasure dome," one sees that it revolves partly round gardens and partly round caverns, rivers, forests, and mountains with "deep romantic chasms"—in short, round what is called Nature. But the whole notion of admiring Nature, and feeling a sort of religious awe in the presence of glaciers, deserts or waterfalls, is bound up with the sense of man's littleness and weakness against the power of the universe. The moon is beautiful partly because we cannot reach it, the sea is impressive because one can never be sure of crossing it

safely. Even the pleasure one takes in a flower—and
this is true even of a botanist who knows all there
is to be known about the flower—is dependent
partly on the sense of mystery. But meanwhile man's
power over Nature is steadily increasing. With the
aid of the atomic bomb we could literally move
mountains: we could even, it is said, alter the cli-
mate of the earth by melting the polar icecaps and
irrigating the Sahara. Isn't there, therefore, something sentimental and obscurantist in preferring
bird-song to swing music and in wanting to leave a
few patches of wildness here and there instead of
covering the whole surface of the earth with a net-
work of Autobahnen flooded by artificial sunlight?

The question only arises because in exploring the
physical universe man has made no attempt to ex-
plore himself. Much of what goes by the name of
pleasure is simply an effort to destroy consciousness.
If one started by asking, What is man? What are
his needs? How can he best express himself? One
would discover that merely having the power to
avoid work and live one's life from birth to death in
electric light and to the tune of tinned music is not
a reason for doing so. Man needs warmth, society,
leisure, comfort, and security: he also needs solitude,
creative work, and the sense of wonder. If he recog-
nized this he could use the products of science and
industrialism eclectically, applying always the same
test: does this make me more human or less human?
He would then learn that the highest happiness

does not lie in relaxing, playing poker, drinking and making love simultaneously. And the instinctive horror which all sensitive people feel at the progressive mechanization of life would be seen not to be a mere sentimental archaism, but to be fully justified. For man only stays human by preserving large patches of simplicity in his life, while the tendency of many modern inventions—in particular the film, the radio and the aeroplane—is to weaken his consciousness, dull his curiosity, and in general drive him nearer to the animals.[9]

What a wonderful statement! How classical in its every inclination, starting with a natural wonder about nature. The one element we have not encountered before concerns the relation between humanism and the scientific conquest of nature. Humanism wants to suit man's full nature, but it is unclear about the relation between man's nature and Nature at large. Linked with a manipulative science, humanism is tempted to assert that Nature at large is not intrinsically admirable or beautiful, and that it can all be altered to suit man's convenience. Natural man in an entirely artificial environment would be the result. To this conception Orwell objects on two grounds. Man cannot fully be himself if he is completely bereft of natural surroundings; in addition, the modern tendency is to narrow and distort the fullness of man's nature in the direction of the most vulgar hedonism. At least one natural object in the humanist scheme must constantly be regarded as intrinsically beautiful and admirable, and that is man. This reflection suggests a danger to which Orwell does not directly refer in his articles but which he later came to appreciate. When all natural objects are looked upon as mere material subject to human manipulation and transformation, can human nature itself continue to be regarded as intrinsically worthy, or will it too become a subject of manipulation? If all other parts of nature lack intrinsic dignity, can man possess it? Certainly if the more vulgar members of the species have their way, those more "comely" attributes of man which are linked to his consciousness may be completely discouraged, and the result of human progress will be to drive man "nearer to the animals." If Orwell knew C. S. Lewis' *The Abolition of Man* he'd say, "Here, here!"

Orwell wants to judge technological advances by their effect on human nature and human life. He speaks of "wanting to leave a few patches of wildness here and there" and of man's need to preserve "large patches of simplicity in his life." These are words of desperation: he senses that the vulgarization of life in advanced societies is well-nigh irresistible. Human nature requires that parts of Nature be kept as objects of intellectual and aesthetic enjoyment—as things to be contemplated, admired, inquired into, or used as models and images in the creative arts. In some of his other writings this attitude can be seen at work more concretely. The protagonist of *Coming Up For Air* (1939), George Bowling, experiences the peak of happiness while gazing, on a warm March day, at some primroses, the burning embers of a wood fire, and a pool covered with duckweed out in the country. He thinks of all the wonderful things in nature and is overcome by wonder and awe:

> Curiously enough, the thing that had suddenly convinced me that life was worth living, more than the

primroses or the young buds on the hedge, was that bit of fire near the gate.... It's curious that a red ember looks more alive, gives you more of a feeling of life, than any living thing.... And I was alive that moment when I stood looking at the primroses and the red embers under the hedge. It's a feeling inside you, a kind of peaceful feeling, and yet it's like a flame.

Farther down the hedge the pool was covered with duckweed, so like a carpet that if you didn't know what duckweed was you might think it was solid and step on it. I wondered why it is that we're all such bloody fools. Why don't people, instead of the idiocies they do spend their time on, just walk round looking at things? That pool, for instance— all the stuff that's in it. Newts, watersnails, water-beetles, caddis-flies, leeches and God knows how many other things that you can only see with a microscope. The mystery of their lives, down there under the water. You could spend a lifetime watching them, ten lifetimes, and still you wouldn't have got to the end even of that one pool. And all the while the sort of feeling of wonder, the peculiar flame inside you. It's the only thing worth having, and we don't want it.[10]

Look at the simple natural things nearby. Consider their mystery. Experience wonder. Bowling goes on to contrast the violence characteristic of war and fascism with such feelings of inner peacefulness. Here again Orwell finds a connection between the height of human happiness and these activities that are uniquely human and derive from the mind itself taken in its natural relation to natural objects. And it is perhaps not accidental that he stresses the satisfactions of observing and wondering rather than those of creativity or even of systematic inquiry into causes. Wonder's beginnings, rather than its completion through philosophy or science, seem more evidently natural and healthful to him. And again, it is perhaps no accident that the natural things immediately around us rather than the starry but distant heavens are what occupy his attention. A certain hesitancy with respect to a science of universal nature may have affected him—a fear that knowledge of nature destroys nature's beauty and admirableness, or may be applied in such a way as to harm natural objects and man himself. In addition, one senses that Orwell placed a higher value on living things—on their motility and variety—than he placed on any inanimate objects whatsoever, including stars and planets. Even sunsets and dawns seem to lack the appeal of primroses, fires (which act alive) and newts.

In general, Orwell views Nature primarily from the standpoint of its value for man—through its ability to engender highly worthwhile human satisfactions—rather than of its value in itself. Were this not the case, his basic position could not be called humanism, and would instead approach the naturalism of Plato and Aristotle. In two newspaper articles written just after the war, this standpoint still predominates, though accompanied by an unmistakable sense of the value possessed by natural things in their own right. One of these articles is devoted to encouraging men to do good for their contemporaries and future generations by planting trees. The other concerns the importance of appreciating the coming of spring, using the renewal processes of the toad as its foremost example.

In it Orwell denies that interest in natural things is either politically or technologically reactionary, or an urbanite luxury:

> I think that by retaining one's childhood love of
> such things as trees, fishes, butterflies and—to re-
> turn to my first instance—toads, one makes a
> peaceful and decent future a little more probable,
> and that by preaching the doctrine that nothing is
> to be admired except steel and concrete, one merely
> makes it a little surer that human beings will have
> no outlet for their surplus energy except in hatred
> and leader-worship.[11]

The reference to childhood suggests that we love living things
for their own sake— an appreciation that is submerged by the
stresses and strains of adult life and especially by the admiration
for the man-made inculcated by a technological society. But
maintaining our natural—i.e., our first and inherent—interest
is the only way to ensure a full and satisfied life, while the frustration of these interests turns us toward such things as hatred
and destructiveness. The idea that the natural is good, as Orwell
employs it, presumes that it is a kind of harmonious working, a
working that keeps harmony within each man and among men.

Free and Equal Brothers

If Orwell was unclear and even inconsistent about the society
that could best bring about human fulfillment, his picture of
the demands of perfect justice among men is less ambiguous.
A good instance can be found in his analysis of Arthur

Koestler's *The Gladiators*, which portrays the attempt of Spartacus' ancient slave rebellion to create a new society, the City of the Sun:

> In this city human beings are to be free and equal, and above all, they are to be happy: no slavery, no hunger, no injustice, no floggings, no executions. It is the dream of a just society which seems to haunt the human imagination ineradicably and in all ages, whether it is called the Kingdom of Heaven or the classless society, or whether it is thought of as a Golden Age which once existed in the past and from which we have degenerated.[12]

This is not the ideal of philosophers, as in Plato's *Republic*, where inequality and limitation in size are found necessary to the establishment of justice. The society Orwell pictures would in its perfected condition be worldwide, constituting a universal brotherhood of all men living without exploiting one another and without laws. This ideal Orwell sometimes regards as arising perennially in protest against social injustice (as above), or sometimes as the product of the Judeo-Christian tradition and, more recently, of the French Revolution and Marxism. In one way or another, these have all contributed to the ideal of human brotherhood, but as Orwell uses it, the conception has reference to a desirable state of affairs in this world, to an "Earthly Paradise." And so self-evidently well-founded does he deem it that thorough argument in its favor is never attempted. The case for it probably begins with the assumption that the central political problem consists in the use of power by some men to exploit others—a practice which is taken to characterize all human history. Within each society there has been economic, social, and political inequality, and among societies inequality, dependence, and exploitation have again been the rule, so that everywhere majorities are underdogs to minorities. The underdog is an innocent victim who finds himself deprived of access to a decent life without just cause. Yet a decent life is good for all men, all desire a life free from insecurity, and only the selfish interests of individuals, classes, and nations prevent these desires from being fulfilled. As long as there are rich and poor, as long as nation is separated from nation, exploitation will go on—hence the need for equality and universality, for a world society. This provision would be ineffective, however, if the ultimate source of inequality lay in the selfish drives of each individual, if men by nature cared naught for their neighbor. But men are not only members of the same biological species. They have more in common than do lions with other lions, or rabbits with other rabbits: they are brothers.

In a sense this is manifestly untrue. Like other animals, men have particular parents, not a single great set of parents. And for one who rejects the Biblical tradition, it is impossible to maintain that God created all men in his own image, wishing them to be brotherly, to love each other. Perhaps, then, Orwell is trying to salvage one part of the Biblical tradition without having recourse to its theological principles. The only natural basis available for such an attempt would seem to be the multitude of particular human families, and no doubt the family plays a fundamental role in Orwell's thought. It is the original and natural social unit, the frame in which love, loyalty, and gratitude first appear as a strong and spontaneous growth. Here is where the joys and sorrows of others are really understood and shared. But the sibling relation—of brothers—is more nearly one of equality than the parent-child relation, and is preferred as the general model for human society because it is closer to the democracy that can alone prevent the exploitation of man by man. And if men are not actually brothers they are in spirit potentially so. The fraternal sympathies which they develop within their particular biological families can be extended, given the proper conditions. England, for example, is such an extended family:

> It has rich relations who have to be kowtowed to and poor relations who are horribly set upon, and there is a deep conspiracy of silence about the source of the family income. It is a family in which the young are generally thwarted and most of the power is in the hands of irresponsible uncles and bedridden aunts. Still, it is a family. It has its private language and its common memories, and at the approach of an enemy it closes its ranks. A family with the wrong members in control—that, perhaps, is as near as one can come to describing England in a phrase.[13]

But men are capable of extending their sympathies beyond patriotism, of recognizing what they have in common with all men, and it is this recognition of a common humanity that would typify the perfect society. No doubt it will vary in its intensity and thoroughness from one individual to another. The majority of men, perhaps, will be capable at most of consideration for the rights of others, of mere sympathy rather than affection and devotion. A few, however, will really care about all mankind in the way a brother, or better still, a mother or father cares. Orwell, it seems, was himself one of these—a man who through direct or sympathetic experience kept putting himself in the place of the underdog masses, the world's victims, and acting on behalf of their just claims. With the help of such intelligent, sensitive, and devoted caretakers, mankind might eventually develop the spirit and institutions making possible a world society of free and equal brothers.

Yet Orwell also admits that human equality and world society were impossible prior to the advent of modern scientific technology. In his natural beginnings, man is impoverished and condemned to brute labor, with only the wealthy finding themselves able to cultivate the higher things. Without man's own technological creativity, the regime of plenty and the communications necessary to the Earthly Paradise could not have come into existence. Unfortunately, the capitalism that created the machine is not its fit manager. With its periodic depressions, its vast economic and social inequalities and its emphasis on private profit rather than brotherliness, capitalism condemns the mass of men to inferiority and exploitation. Marxists, on the other hand, are all too frequently dedicated to envying and hating the bourgeoisie, and to extreme abstract programs rather than the real welfare of the people. What is most needed, therefore, is a humanized liberal socialism which will make justice, freedom, decency and the common good its real goals and strive to become a world system.

This is the general picture that one can compose on the basis of the two works in which Orwell speaks most explicitly of his socialist aims: *The Road to Wigan Pier* (1937) and *The*

Lion and the Unicorn (1941). Only in this way, he claims (during the war), can fascism's tremendously aggressive menace to human equality be overcome. Since the old order is unjust to so many, since the technological conditions are immediately available by which the just socialist order can be instituted and rendered stable, and since the threat of fascism cannot otherwise be averted, there is a right and duty to overthrow the fundamental institution of private property together with its domestic and foreign exploitations, replacing it with state ownership controlled by and run for the people. These political views both in their general form and particular application are highly questionable. Does Orwell himself correct them?

Critique of Power Politics

Although Orwell begins as a supporter of both the desirability and possibility of the Earthly Paradise, he usually denies that its coming is a matter of historic necessity, in this way departing from orthodox Marxism. He explicitly distinguishes his own position from the typical liberal attitude in two vital respects: he has a much higher estimate of the power of sheer passion and prejudice, and he claims that the admiration of force and fraud has come to characterize a sizeable number of the intellectuals themselves.

The social-scientific hedonists—of whom H. G. Wells is the leading example—regard motivations other than enlightened self-interest and social interest as doomed to extinction in the age of modern science. They neither appeal to, nor see, the tremendous strength of such emotions as patriotism, superstition, traditionalism. They do not realize that:

The energy that actually shapes the world springs from emotions—racial pride, leader-worship, religious belief, love of war—which liberal intellectuals write off as anachronisms, and which they have usually destroyed so completely in themselves as to have lost all power of action.[14]

And again:

He (H. G. Wells) was, and still is, quite incapable of understanding that nationalism, religious bigotry, and feudal loyalty are far more powerful forces than what he himself would describe as sanity.[15]

Orwell tries to base his own politics on the necessity and usefulness of some of these emotions. His call for a Socialist revolution in England in *The Lion and the Unicorn* is developed in conjunction with a first-rate analysis of English national character. For the most part he finds the beliefs and emotions underlying this character morally admirable—e.g., the defensive patriotic loyalty, the gentleness, the trust in liberty and law, the deep Christian decency. Whereas the tendency of English left-wing intellectuals is to "chip away" at patriotism and the martial virtues, Orwell claims that these are absolutely essential both to the survival of England in its war against Hitler and to its turning toward Socialism.

The essay called "Notes on Nationalism" (1945) begins by distinguishing nationalism from patriotism:

By "patriotism" I mean devotion to a particular place and a particular way of life, which one believes to

be the best in the world but has no wish to force
upon other people. Patriotism is of its nature defensive, both militarily and culturally. Nationalism,
on the other hand, is inseparable from the desire for
power. The abiding purpose of every nationalist is
to secure more power and more prestige, not for
himself but for the nation or other unit in which he
has chosen to sink his own individuality.

   ...Nationalism, in the extended sense in which I
am using the word, includes such movements and
tendencies as Communism, political Catholicism,
Zionism, anti-Semitism, Trotzkyism, and Pacifism.[16]

According to Orwell, the most worrisome trait of the twentieth
century is the growing strength of nationalism and the relative
weakening of moral, religious, and patriotic restraints. The development of Nazi and Communist totalitarian tyrannies ruth-
lessly using fraud and force for their own aggrandizement has
been accompanied by a growth among intellectuals everywhere
of "realism"—the doctrine that might is right, the admiration
of power, cruelty, and wickedness for their own sake. Orwell
continually contrasts the common people of the Western coun-
tries (and especially of England) who are "still living in the
world of absolute good and evil," "the mental world of Dickens,"
with those intellectuals who have gone over to realism, power-
politics, power-worship, and totalitarianism, whether of the Left
or Right. These intellectuals have become the slaves of some aggressive orthodoxy, promoting its interest by every means and
regarding all questions in the light of their bearing on these interests. So great is the degree to which falsification for one's

own side is engaged in that Orwell fears "…that the very concept of objective truth is fading out of the world." As applied to history, "…what is peculiar to our own age is the abandonment of the idea that history could be truthfully written."[17] In England it is the mythos of Russian Communism that has become the major nationalism of the intellectuals and the one most in need of being combatted. Hence the paradox that the very people who require freedom most, and whose intelligence might qualify them to be the deliverers of mankind, comprise the totalitarian vanguard. The extreme wing of Social-Scientific hedonism stands for tyranny rather than democracy.

Orwell speculates about the causes of the growth of Communist sympathies among English intellectuals. Especially since about 1930, English society was able to offer them little status. The rationalistic debunking of "patriotism, religion, the Empire, the family" also prompted them to turn elsewhere for something to believe in. Many were led by a strong desire for power or for association with power capable of getting its dictates obeyed. And there were, of course, those who were attracted by Communist slogans only because a comfortable and safe life in England and an ignorance of the special horrors of totalitarianism lulled them into doing so. As we have already seen, Orwell thought there was a causal connection between the decline of religious belief and the rise of modern power worship. It is the "emancipated" intellects who are attracted to a secular religion embodying and wielding power, and this fact added to Orwell's appreciation of the weighty merits of the "old regime"—of patriotism, the code of the gentleman, and even religion.[18] But what he actually calls for to combat the nationalism of the intellectuals is a moral effort on the part of every man to reduce

his own biases and strive for greater objectivity and fairness—
admittedly an effort few seem to be capable of putting forth.
His final resort, in other words, is simply to moral exhortation.[19]

The essay on nationalism seems to make two related points:
first, that the confidence in objective standards of truth and
morality is disappearing; second, that popular emotions and beliefs objectionable from the standpoint of rationality are crucial
to practical life and hence to liberalism. He would have found
an ally in Edmund Burke, to whom he never refers. Against
these trends, Orwell upholds the possibility of historical truth
and insists that there is a vital moral distinction between defensive and aggressive loyalties or devotions to a cause. But he
does not go further in defending the ethics he upholds. He certainly does not speak of duties or rights, virtues or vices: he does
not employ the vocabulary of either practical moral discourse
or philosophy. The common people still believe in "absolute
good and evil," in the moral world of Charles Dickens, but Orwell's language suggests that he himself actually shares the
doubts of the intellectuals and is torn between the two.

Increasing Pessimism

Almost unwaveringly, Orwell holds to the desirability of the
Earthly Paradise and to its need for controlling technological
advance in a manner appropriate to the full complement of
man's needs. But he does waver considerably on the likelihood
of its coming. Most of the time he maintains that both liberal
socialism and the totalitarian slave state can produce stable social systems, and that both are equal possibilities. Sometimes
he expresses confidence in the ultimate victory of a reasonable

scientifically-planned society and of the common man.[20] Sometimes he is so struck by the increasing might of totalitarianism as to admit that "…almost certainly we are moving into an age of totalitarian dictatorship—an age in which freedom of thought will be at first a deadly sin and later on a meaningless expression."[21]

The state of Orwell's thought toward the end of the war can best be seen in his essay on Arthur Koestler and in *Animal Farm*. On the whole, he admires Koestler, agreeing with him as to the desirability of the Earthly Paradise and sympathizing with his view that revolutions necessarily lead to something like the Russian system, that "…all efforts to regenerate society by violent means lead to the cellars of the OGPU."[22] The world since 1930 has given every reason for pessimism rather than optimism: things are getting much worse instead of much better. But he cannot accept Koestler's renunciation of revolutionary activity, which he traces directly to the latter's inability to accept misery as an inherent and sizeable portion of human life.

> The real problem is how to restore the religious attitude while accepting death as final. Men can only be happy when they do not assume that the object of life is happiness. It is most unlikely, however, that Koestler would accept this. There is a well-marked hedonistic strain in his writings, and his failure to find a political position after breaking with Stalinism is a result of this.[23]

Orwell then proceeds to re-state the need for revolution on the basis of this less sanguine view of human possibilities:

Perhaps, however, whether desirable or not, it (the
Earthly Paradise) isn't possible. Perhaps some degree of suffering is inevitable. Perhaps the choice
before man is always a choice of evils, perhaps even
the aim of Socialism is not to make the world perfect but to make it better. All revolutions are failures, but they are not all the same failure. It is his
unwillingness to admit this that has led Koestler's
mind temporarily into a blind alley....[24]

The use of "perhaps" in this passage unintentionally but
strikingly testifies to the boundless confidence in social transformation characteristic of both Marxism and mainline liberalism in the nineteenth and twentieth centuries. By contrast,
patience in the face of ineradicable suffering is called a "religious attitude" rather than simple common sense. But Orwell's
detractions from the optimism of social-scientific hedonism
and his belated concessions to common sense cannot consistently lead to a new revolutionary position if Koestler's analysis
of the consequences of violent revolution is true, and Orwell
had as much as granted its truth. If violent revolution must result in tyranny, no revolution is justified. This is probably why
Animal Farm, published the following year, seems to accept
Koestler's analysis *in toto*. *Animal Farm* has been widely interpreted as a satire on Russian Communism, and no doubt much
of its material is based on the events of the Bolshevik revolution. Nevertheless, the circumstances of the animal revolution
for the sake of an Earthly Paradise are depicted in a quite generalized manner, as if to say that any violent revolution would
in all probability end in tyranny. The whole point of the book

is that revolutions bring to the fore men of ruthlessness and cunning whose moral defects lead them to seize upon opportunities for domination and ultimately to establish a regime much worse than the one revolted against.

In Orwell's view the opposite of revolutionary activity is the conscious, pessimistic abstention from politics, or "quietism." In spite of his numerous injunctions against this kind of withdrawal, there are two important places where he shows sympathy for it. The first occurs in the essay "Inside the Whale" (1940), where a survey of the development of English literature in his own lifetime is used in analyzing Henry Miller's novels. As Orwell sees it, Miller's quietism represents the human voice speaking in an age of disintegration, of growing totalitarianism, and "…in the remaining years of free speech any novel worth reading will follow more or less along the lines that Miller has followed."[25] The second instance is the sympathetic portrait of Benjamin the Jackass in *Animal Farm*. Benjamin is a morose and silent animal, intelligent, desirous of living long, and devoted to his friends. But he is entirely without optimism concerning the alleviation of suffering through any kind of political action, and simply goes about minding his own business.

In his own life Orwell was never capable of remaining quiet. The year after "Inside the Whale," his strongest call to Socialist revolution, was published and later, in 1947, he refers to himself as primarily a "political writer," attempting in *Animal Farm* and its sequel (*1984*) to combine political opposition to totalitarianism and support for democratic socialism with artistic purpose. These later writings, in other words, may be viewed as efforts to disprove his earlier contention that only literature like Miller's was still conceivable in a pre-totalitarian age. The ideal to which Orwell remains true was the one he found in the person of Charles Dickens, about whom he wrote (the year before he wrote on Miller) that one imagines his face to be that:

> ...of a man who is always fighting against something, but who fights in the open and is not frightened, the face of a man who is generously angry—in other words, of a nineteenth-century liberal, a free intelligence, a type hated with equal hatred by all the smelly little orthodoxies which are now contending for our souls.[26]

Orwell would not surrender his soul to these orthodoxies, to the intellectuals who have abandoned intellect. Even as late as 1948 he insists that the intellectual, the writer, cannot keep out of politics in an age so politically turbulent and so inundated by political influence as the contemporary one. The material forming his own experience is largely determined by politics. In addition, his own freedom as a writer is at stake in the political battles of the day. Furthermore,

> ...we have developed a sort of compunction which our grandparents did not have, an awareness of the enormous injustice and misery of the world, and a guilt-stricken feeling that one ought to be doing something about it...[27]

Orwell therefore supports not only the writer's participation in politics but also his use of political subject matter in literary writings, provided that he constantly attempts to reveal the truth as he sees it, undistorted by the requirements of any political dogma whatsoever.

Broadly speaking, and not without backslidings, Orwell's thought develops from an early confidence that political action can bring about socialism to a later despair concerning the possibility of even preventing totalitarianism from dominating the world, much less of establishing socialism. Regardless of its impracticability, however, the struggle to ameliorate human suffering must be maintained. Without saying so, Orwell seems to have taken upon himself and all men the overwhelming burden of responsibility the Biblical tradition attributes to God alone.

On His Predecessors

Orwell's remarks about those of his immediate predecessors who wrote Utopian or anti-Utopian novels or made large-scale predictions about the future are of great importance in understanding *1984*. The authors he mentions are H. G. Wells, Jack London, Hilaire Belloc, Zamyatin, Aldous Huxley, and James Burnham. As we have already seen, he sides with Huxley against H. G. Wells' social-scientific hedonism. Nevertheless he considers both fundamentally defective in their predictions about the future of mankind. Instead of Well's technologically-based hedonism of free men or Huxley's technologically-based hedonism of slaves, a brutal tyranny in the fascist and communist mold is probable.

Orwell's book review of Zamyatin's *We* (1946) is largely devoted to comparing it with Huxley's *Brave New World*.

Both books deal with the rebellion of the primitive
human spirit against a rationalized, mechanized
painless world, and both stories are supposed to
take place about six hundred years hence.[28]

Both picture a world in which happiness is achieved at the
price of freedom, but Zamyatin's is "on the whole more relevant
to our own situation," first, because such "primitive" or "ancient"
human instincts as maternal feeling, sexual love, and the desire
for liberty have not been removed from the population by scientific manipulation; second, because the motivation attributed
to the rulers is sounder. Whereas Huxley does not make this
motivation clear (e.g., neither economic exploitation nor
power-hunger seems to be their objective), Zamyatin does
grasp "the irrational side of totalitarianism—human sacrifice,
cruelty as an end in itself, the worship of a leader who is cred-
ited with divine attributes…." Orwell concludes by noting that
"What Zamyatin seems to be targeting is not any particular
country but the implied aims of industrial civilization," and
that "…he had a strong leaning toward primitivism." In effect,
We is "…a study of the Machine, the genie that man has
thoughtlessly let out of its bottle and cannot put back again."

While Huxley and Zamyatin write about a rather distant fu-
ture, James Burnham describes the revolutions now occurring in
Western civilization and is concerned with shorter-term trends.
In an essay appearing a few months later than the above review,
Orwell states his reactions to Burnham's outlook. As he sees it,
Burnham proposes a general Machiavellian view of the history
of human societies, an interpretation of the present that accords
with that view, and corresponding directives for action. All history

is and must remain the history of class domination. All political rule must be oligarchical and must involve force and fraud. Promises of democracy and human brotherhood are meant only to lead the unpolitical masses into action for a cause not really their own. Today, capitalism is doomed, and not free socialism but oligarchical, state-controlled "managerialism" of the Nazi and Communist kind is replacing it. A few such super-states will divide the world among themselves and then endure, and the only practical action is to cooperate with and guide this process.

Orwell agrees with Burnham that capitalism is disappearing and doomed, and that managerialism is on the rise "…if one considers the world-movement as a whole…." But he rejects the oligarchical law of history and the acceptance of the need for political immorality as distinguished from private morality. Modern technology makes possible the existence of a moral political order, a Socialist democracy, whereas in earlier times "… class divisions were not only unavoidable, but desirable" for the progress of civilization. At the same time Orwell denies that a Nazi or Communist oligarchy built on continuing force and fraud can last, arguing that "…certain rules of conduct have to be observed if human society is to hold together at all," and that "…slavery is no longer a stable basis for human society." He criticizes the "realism" of Burnham and the "managers," using the latter term to refer (at least in the English case) to "scientists, technicians, teachers, journalists, broadcasters, bureaucrats, professional politicians." These are the middling people who admire totalitarian success, power, and cruelty and would like to share in it themselves. Burnham's moral defects ruin his forecasting power by biasing him against democracy and in favor of totalitarianism. His fundamental error is an inability to realize that totalitarianism is wicked and should be fought to the death. Accordingly, his arguments against the possibility of democratic Socialism and his prediction of an inevitable, enduring tripartite oligarchical division of the world are badly in error.[29]

It is somewhat disconcerting to see Orwell criticize Burnham for the thought that totalitarianism can endure, since he did not find the same thought defective in Zamyatin, and had, in fact, frequently expressed it himself. As his treatment of Koestler has already revealed, he was at times given to impulsive reaction when some of his own basic premises were directly threatened. Koestler had jeopardized the desirability of revolution, Burnham both the desirability and possibility of the Earthly Paradise. But just as further reflection must have convinced Orwell to adopt Koestler's thesis in *Animal Farm*, so it must also have convinced him—and only shortly afterward—to adopt Burnham's analysis of history and forecast of the future in *1984*. Yet he refuses to accept the latter's Machiavellianism, and in fact writes to oppose, and help others oppose, the probable or inevitable spread of totalitarianism.

This concludes our survey of Orwell's main moral and political views prior to *1984*. There are occasionally inconsistencies. They are presented in many different forms and places. Even so, there is a remarkable depth, steadiness, and unity in the problems he addressed, and his most complex, most mature, and final writing must be understood as an attempt to draw his questions and answers together into an intelligible synthesis. What should we do? Why should we be? What is to become of mankind? Where will his deeper understanding of the depths and heights of humanity lead him?

Part Two
The Teaching of Good and Evil in *1984*

Plan of the Work

The novel *1984* deals with a small-scale rebellion against a perfected tyranny in the year of its title. Its three major chapters bear only stark numerical headings, as do their several subsections. Its development is simple. In One, Winston Smith's defiance of the regime begins. In Two, Winston has an illicit love affair with Julia and both decide to join up with what they take to be an underground revolutionary organization—the Brotherhood—shortly thereafter being captured by the Thought Police. In Three, O'Brien casts off his disguise as a leader of the Brotherhood and proceeds, in his real capacity as Inner Party leader, to force the two rebels into orthodoxy.

Corresponding to these three stages of the revolt are three stages in Winston's education concerning the regime. In One he is seen learning on his own, in Two he is assisted by Julia and the Brotherhood's textbook, and in Three his instructor becomes O'Brien. Whereas only the "how" of the total tyranny is presented in the first two chapters, the third divulges the ultimate motives of the ruling few—their "why." The education of the reader, however, is capable of exceeding that of Winston. Orwell supplies the reader not only with a direct view of the conscious states of his characters—what they observe, feel, think, read, will—but also with descriptions of their inner and outer condition and environment. The author's role, accordingly, is that of an on-the-spot witness privileged with the power of observing both from within and without. And as a witness he refrains from making overt evaluations. The single departure from this stance of the non-evaluating contemporary of the action occurs in the appendix dealing with the "Principles of Newspeak," where a comparison of the old with the new language is included in an analysis of the latter's aims and methods. Otherwise, the reader lives with the author and his creations in the imagined future. Thus, by reflecting on all the material furnished by the author, the reader can see more than the characters themselves and seek the view of human affairs woven into the whole.

Winston's Situation

Let us reconstruct the setting in which Winston finds himself. He lives in London, the main city of Airstrip One and part of Oceania, one of the three super-powers controlling the entire world. The real rulers of the state are Big Brother and the Inner Party, assisted by the Outer Party, while the proles or laboring class have no part in governing at all. But the Outer Party too is far more governed than governing: it is only the instrument for carrying out decisions made by the Inner Party, and because of its position and talents requires to be under greater surveillance than the proles. In general, by conscious plan, the lives of the ruled are so manipulated that not only the opportunity for revolting but its very thought is practically eliminated. The main technique used by the regime is to generate opinions and emotions that render the ruled either harmless to the state or its fervent supporters—i.e., either indifferent or pursuing its purposes as the greatest of all goods. Aided by advanced technology, scientific study, and a variety of institutions, the regime produces a unique amalgam of fear for one's own preservation and distrust of others, on the one hand, with enthusiasm for communal undertakings, on the other. At the same time that the individual feels completely isolated and menaced he participates in the tremendous onrushing of the state's activities. War, hate orgies, telescreens, planned changes in language, chastity leagues, novel-writing machines, arbitrary arrests, child spies and so forth are all part of the elaborate system of control. But the crowning instrument for glorifying the regime involves "Doublethink" and the "Mutability of the Past." By their means, the human intellect is trained into utter subservience to the dictates of the Inner Party, and comes to believe true that which the Party stipulates, regardless of evidence and opinions to the contrary known to it. The Party's claim to infallibility is accepted, and once regarded as the supreme source of wisdom and goodness as well as power, it is beyond overthrow.

How is Revolt Possible?

Nevertheless, Winston rebels. What prompts him to do so? After about twenty years in power, the regime had come to be taken by most as part of the natural order of things. Within so closed a system, how could Winston raise questions concerning its validity? He does so, first of all, out of discontent with the frenzies, pains, fears, and hatred which he experiences in himself and observes in others. In addition, he discerns vast gaps between realities and what the regime claims to have accomplished or claims to be true. Finally, he has both present and remembered experiences of things which strike him as being greatly superior in some way to what the regime provides both in theory and practice. The first constitutes primarily an experience of the bad, the second of the false, the third of the good. Here are some illustrations from the text:

> In the Two Minutes Hate he could not help sharing in the general delirium, but this subhuman chanting of "B-B...B-B!" always filled him with horror.[30]
>
> How could you tell how much of it was lies? It might be true that the average human being was better off now than he had been before the Revolution. The only evidence to the contrary was the mute protest in your bones, the instinctive feeling that the conditions you lived in were intolerable and that at some other time they must have been different. It struck him that the truly characteristic thing about modern life was not its cruelty and insecurity, but simply its bareness, its dinginess, its listlessness. Life, if you looked about you, bore no resemblance not only to the lies that streamed out of the telescreens, but even to the ideals that the Party was trying to achieve.[31]
>
> Everything faded into mist. The past was erased, the erasure was forgotten, the lie became truth. Just once in his life he had possessed—after the event: that was what counted—concrete, unmistakable evidence of an act of falsification.[32]

...but the room had awakened in him a sort of nostalgia, a sort of ancestral memory. It seemed to him that he knew exactly what it felt like to sit in a room like this, in an armchair beside an open fire with your feet on the fender and a kettle on the hob, utterly alone, utterly secure, with nobody watching you, no voice pursuing you....[33]

But by degrees the flood of music drove all speculations out of his mind. It was as though it were a kind of liquid stuff that poured all over him and got mixed up with the sunlight that filtered through the leaves. He stopped thinking and merely felt.[34]

In general, Winston can dissent from the way of life extolled by the regime because he is still somehow capable of thoughts and feelings which it does not control. He begins to regard as bad and deserving of avoidance those things which bring him dissatisfaction, as good and worthy of being sought those things which satisfy him. What he desires, likes, admires, does naturally, spontaneously, from sources within himself, rather than what the regime dictates, becomes his guiding standard.

Nature and the Good

To demonstrate this turning to what is ultimately an identification of the good with what is natural to man, we shall examine Winston's two dream sequences and several other particulars as well. The first dream[35] contains four central ideas: his mother's sacrificing her life for his when he was a child; a rural scene which he calls the Golden Country; a girl (Julia) splendidly flinging off her clothes as she approaches him; finally, the word "Shakespeare." The second dream[36] is an elaboration upon the "mother" theme alone and serves to give further emphasis to the love and willingness to sacrifice which she brought to her children. In both cases, her natural, private feelings are viewed with admiration. Having given birth to her offspring, she cares for them, whereas, in contrast, the regime sacrifices its subjects to its own good.

The Golden Country represents a reaction to the city that the regime constructs and controls. The rabbits, the hedge, the trees, the wind, the stream and fish are exemplars of the nature that pre-dates the regime and has not been distorted by it. They symbolize an earlier, simpler, and happier existence, and are depicted in a state of rest and movement which is essentially peaceful. Again, the girl's proud disrobing retrieves for physical beauty and sexual desire their natural and proper place in human life, in contrast to the sexual antipathies promoted by the regime. The word "Shakespeare" sums up the loyalties and loves belonging to the "ancient time" as well as the sense of tragedy they make possible. Intended as an actual reminiscence of Winston's childhood, it serves to epitomize what has been lost in Oceania and all that we have referred to earlier as Orwell's humanistic philosophy. To find a source of opposition to Oceania's artificial re-molding of men, Orwell has recourse to the natural elements of human life and, in particular, to the emotions and "private loyalties" of the "ancient time." Paradoxically, however, the "ancient time" refers not to man's earliest beginnings but to the period immediately preceding Oceania—i.e., to the period of capitalistic democracy. Man's original nature seems to have expressed itself most fully in highly developed "bourgeois" society! Liberalism's philosopher John Locke would have been proud.

Orwell treats several kinds of social attachment as natural to man. The object of the attachment can either be particular (as with familial and sexual love, and friendship) or general (as in the case of sympathy). The proles are models of sympathy, and Winston's first diary entrance is an account of an atrocity film to which a female prole makes animated objection. Later, Winston instinctively moves forward to help the fallen Julia, even though he then believes her to be a threat to his life. Still later, he remembers kicking a human limb (after the explosion of a robot bomb) "…as if it had been a cabbage stalk." He realizes that:

> The proles had stayed human. They had not become hardened inside. They had held onto the primitive emotions which he himself had to relearn by conscious effort.[37]

And there is evidence that if men had some real contact with those beyond their national boundaries, their sympathy for such strangers would be activated. We should add the fact that Winston himself is able to expand his natural sympathy into a conscious care for "the human heritage" and the decent future of all mankind. On the relation between this and parental (especially maternal) affection we have already dwelled. Winston's rebellion for the sake of mankind is modeled on the care his mother bestowed upon him during his childhood. To wreck this devotion and loyalty, as well as the affection and loyalty that has sprung up between Winston and Julia, is O'Brien's

foremost aim in the final chapter. Of ordinary friendship there
are no eminent examples in the work, the closest to it being
Winston's links with Mr. Charrington and O'Brien, both of
whom betray him. In the area of individual social attachments,
therefore, the work gives special importance to maternal rather
than paternal love, and to the intimate sharing of sexual love
rather than friendship.

The intellect's striving for truth is another element of
human nature on which the novel as a whole focuses, and it is
shown to have a vital bearing on man's sociality as well. The
Party demands Doublethink and controls the evidence which
might permit the truth to be ascertained at the same time that
it controls the minds and persons of the ruled:

> The Party told you to reject the evidence of your
> eyes and ears. It was their final, most essential com-
> mand.... And yet he was in the right! They were
> wrong and he was right. The obvious, the silly and
> the true had got to be defended. Truisms are true,
> hold on to that![38]

What Winston does is to defend the natural capacity of the
human mind for knowledge, pitting the inner cognition against
the external command. By his nature, man can know. On the
most elementary level, this is seen in the consciousness of his
own feelings, sensations, memories, and so on which Winston
experiences and is able to communicate to a large degree, even
if his isolation actually prevents him from doing so. But Winston also recognizes his own mental limitations in terms of the
evidence he lacks, the things he does not remember, the

observations he cannot explain: hence his overpowering desire to procure evidence and talk with other men. He attempts to converse with an old prole about pre-revolutionary times. He enjoys Mr. Charrington's openness, and seeks to further his understanding through discussions with Julia and the Brotherhood's book. A large part of O'Brien's fatal attraction for Winston, in fact, lies in his seeming to be a man who could be spoken to and who could understand.

1984 as a whole assumes that at least some parts of reality are accessible to human knowing. Through his mind, man is linked with the knowable, and, through speech, with other potential sharers of knowledge, who are also needed for the cognitive process itself. And by the very character of the goal—i.e., truth—there must be no violence here. By being that which uniquely corresponds to the reality it attempts to describe, truth is one and the same for all men and the ground of ultimate agreement amongst them. But men will frequently disagree about it. O'Brien and Winston unite in defining truth as correctness of assertion about reality. For O'Brien, however, realities and their corresponding truths are made and unmade by decision of the Inner Party, while for Winston they are independent of all human fiat. Around this difference are constructed some of the final arguments between the two in the torture chambers of the Ministry of Love.

The first of the two dreams occurs to Winston when he is home in bed near the beginning of the novel, the second when he and Julia fall asleep in their hideaway. In between,[39] his first rendezvous with Julia out in the countryside takes place, and here the second and third parts of the first dream are actualized: the setting is just like the Golden Country, and Julia disrobes with the same abandon as the girl in the dream. But the rendezvous scene contains several additional elements as well. Julia offers Winston a piece of chocolate of the pre-war variety which proves delightful to the taste and at the same time stirs up in him some "powerful and troubling" memory (of his mother's devotion and his own youthful selfishness) which only the second dream brings to full consciousness. The second additional element consists of the thrush's joyous and free outpouring of song by which Winston is filled with pure pleasure. And Winston's exulting in the sex-urge—"the animal instinct, the simple undifferentiated desire"—is the third. In all three we again see Orwell employing the standard of that which men enjoy, seek, or do by nature, apart from convention and compulsion. The pleasures of tasting chocolate, listening to the thrush's music, and engaging in sexual intercourse—enjoyed in a natural setting—are used to epitomize successful rebellion. The inner happiness that comes from the fulfillment of natural capacities and needs is what the tyranny fears most. Unlike the thrush, the Party members never sing "alone and spontaneously": "The birds sing, the proles sang, the Party did not sing."[40]

What we have said so far about Orwell's portrayal of man's social, intellectual, and physical needs is by no means exhaustive of the book's details. There are, in addition, numerous indications of the body's natural need for decent food, health, freedom from pain, and proper relaxation, and of the mind's need to do its own work in an atmosphere of encouragement. Further attention is also given to Winston's aesthetic responses. Among women he finds beauty in Julia, in his mother, in prole wives, and he is especially affected by the appearance of the diary book and glass paperweight he discovers in Mr. Charrington's shop. But our general point is already sufficiently clear: through concrete example rather than discursive reasoning, Orwell's *1984* seeks to elaborate that comprehensive view of human nature which is the basis of the humanist ethics so urgently needed in the modern world.

Evil

We can now show that, in Orwell's view, external factors frustrating or distorting human nature are responsible for men being or doing evil. A useful point of departure is the institution called the Two Minutes Hate. Working through certain naturally painful or disquieting sensations and through the natural desires for self-preservation and security, the Hate arouses "a hideous ecstasy of fear and vindictiveness, a desire to kill, to torture, to smash faces in with a sledge hammer...."[41] and eventually generates dependence upon the strength of Big Brother. Here the participant is himself harmed, and prepared for the harming of others, through the artificial exaggeration of his natural self-interest and the systematic weakening of his rational and sympathetic capacities.

The regime's treatment of the sexual urge is another case in point. By putting a premium on chastity, it generates anxieties and destructive energies that can be used for political purposes. Winston is shown in three kinds of sexual relationship—first with his wife Katherine, then with an aged prostitute, and finally with Julia. The first two prove to be unsatisfactory and frustrating in the extreme. Katherine has had her natural desires trained out of her by the party and is no longer capable of sexual reciprocity. And in the same way that she typifies the politicization of sexuality, the prostitute typifies its commercialization. The degradation of the latter relation—especially in the view of the advanced age of the prostitute—serves only to increase Winston's frustration, and this thwarting of his sexual and affectionate nature results in a will to do violence. The theme of frustration issuing in hatred and the desire to hurt appears, in fact, in several places.

The state of Winston's drinking and of his varicose ulcer figures prominently as the barometer of his general well-being. During his affair with Julia, his previously strong addiction to alcohol tends to disappear:

> Winston had dropped his habit of drinking gin at all hours. He seemed to have lost the need for it. He had grown fatter, his varicose ulcer had subsided, leaving only a brown stain on the skin above the ankle, his fits of coughing in the early morning had stopped.[42]

But following his final defeat by O'Brien, both ailments reappear. Other illustrations of the same general idea are the use of fear to eliminate normal confidence and friendship, the training of the young to spy on and betray their parents, and Julia's one-sided concentration on the pleasures of sex in defiance of the regime's prohibitions. Just as the proper functioning of man's nature is accompanied by pleasure, satisfaction, peacefulness, happiness, so its improper function is accompanied by pain, anxiety, violence, and misery.

The Highest Human Type

Thus far, the various natural capacities and needs have been regarded as identical in all men and as of equal worth with each other. But men vary, they must frequently choose between conflicting natural desires, and they do not seem to know by nature the proper quantity and order of their natural satisfactions. There is much evidence in *1984* that these issues greatly occupied Orwell, for without a solution to them no humanist ethic can stand. To mention only one instance: the scene in Room 101 represents a conflict between Winston's desire for his own preservation and his love for Julia—i.e., between two natural tendencies. We must therefore examine the text for Orwell's solution to the problem of the proper or best order of man's natural parts.

In general the characters of *1984* may be said to fall into two main groups, one approved by Orwell, the other condemned by him. In the first we have Winston himself, his mother, Julia, the proles, Mr. Charrington, Goldstein (as known through his treatise), and O'Brien in his role as rebel leader. The second is constituted by Parsons, Syme, Katherine, Ampleforth, and their like in the Outer Party and by O'Brien in the Inner Party. For it the power and ways of the regime furnish the ultimate standard of worth. The stupid Parsons and Katherine work for the regime through non-intellectual means, and derive satisfaction from serving it and from the prestige of serving it. Syme and Ampleforth, on the other hand, found their destinies on special intellectual work in its service. All are its creatures both by having been in large degree molded by it and by their continuing devotion to it. To O'Brien and the

Inner Party they are related as slave to master, since the former
are the regime that is glorified and served. O'Brien himself can
therefore be considered the perfection of this group: he represents the regime they admire, and he is that regime by virtue
not only of his position in the Inner Party but of his fully understanding what the regime signifies.[43]

The members of Winston's group are either less affected
by the regime or in conscious revolt against it. In order to discover their merits and deficiencies, recourse must be had to
Winston's appraisals of them. To begin with, it is clear that he
regards O'Brien the rebel as the highest human type within
his experience. From the outset he sees in him a highly intelligent and public-spirited, strong and courageous, yet fundamentally gentle and peaceful man. O'Brien has a charm, a
curiously civilized manner, an appearance of inner control and
self-sufficiency, a sense of the humorous. He can be talked to,
can understand, and for this reason is made the addressee of
Winston's secret diary. In fact, his intellectual sociality is a trait
Winston continues to admire even after discovering his real
identity and being tortured by him. As rebel leader, therefore,
he seems to be the personification of what might be called the
heroic, civilized man, and Goldstein's treatise looks like the
kind of document that might appropriately issue from him.

Judged by the type of O'Brien-Goldstein, the proles, Julia,
and Winston himself are all in one way or another deficient.
First the proles: human in feeling, strong in body, sane, preserving family life and serving society through their labor, they
are regarded by Winston as immortal and as the eventual sav-
iors of Oceania. Yet they are also lacking in intelligence, pub-
lic-spiritedness, and charm and, beyond their work and family

concerns, occupy themselves only with petty amusements and disputes. As for Julia, she is loved by Winston but only partly admired. Her devotion to him and her practical shrewdness do not compensate for the fact that she is "only a rebel from the waist downward." Unlike Winston, her concern does not extend to the next generation or to all men, and she has neither the capacity nor the desire to understand the regime thoroughly. But Winston acknowledges his own defects relative to the proles, to Julia, and to O'Brien-Goldstein. He calls Goldstein's treatise "…the product of a mind similar to his own, but enormously more powerful, more systematic, less fear-ridden." He envies Julia's practicality. And just as he feels a "mystical reverence" for the singing prole mother, he experiences "a wave of admiration, almost of worship" in the presence of O'Brien the rebel leader—in both cases sensing a strength which must ultimately triumph over the hated regime.[44]

If rebel O'Brien is meant to embody Orwell's conception of the highest human type—the type of the heroic, civilized man—in what sense can that type also be called natural? For there are two immediate difficulties to be overcome: are O'Brien's traits natural or acquired, and how can one human being serve as the model for all others, given the natural diversity of human beings? In addition, there is the ultimate question as to why this precise set of traits must be accounted the highest. Here we begin to run short of evidence in the text, for Orwell does not show the degree to which nature, training, and experience joined together in forming O'Brien's qualities, and the few things we do learn about children (Winston's own childhood and Parson's two children) indicate only that there are certain elementary ingredients of upbringing required for the

production of all decent human beings. It is clear that an unusual natural intelligence is needed, but whether such things as
devotion to others, strength of character and body, grace, and
charm have their basis in unusual natural gifts or in training
does not become clear. In fact, these constituents of O'Brien's
makeup would seem to be separable one from the other rather
than inherently clustered together, as is shown by the fact that
Winston is unusually devoted to mankind but not conspicuous
for strength or grace. Indeed, O'Brien himself is portrayed as
possessing not a beautiful but an ugly face (like Socrates of
yore)—as if to emphasize the fact that the various desirable
traits do not all come together. Their uniting in a single individual, then, would seem in part to be a matter of chance.

But what is it that makes this particular set of characteristics desirable and somehow more natural to man than any
other? We must speculate since Orwell himself does not speak
explicitly on this crucial point. There is a certain coherence in
the features attributed to rebel O'Brien. They are, first of all,
uniquely human, rather than traits man shares with the brutes.
The model man is not selected on the basis of the efficiency of
his digestive system, his sexual prowess, the accuracy of his
senses, or even his athletic ability. The traits so deeply admired
by Winston, though only partly possessed by him, have their
seat in intellect and sociality: these are what make a man
human. There also seems to be a connection between O'Brien's
intellect and both his strength of character and body and his
grace and charm. Intellect appears to rule in O'Brien in the full
sense, guiding his feeling and action as well as his thought. It
resists his being swayed this way and that by external force or
blind emotion. It provides his independence and strength, but

also his gentleness. It lends grace and charm to his presence. It evokes his noble dedication to human good. Above all, it permits him to be truly "civilized"—i.e., the opposite of subhuman, savage, bestial, or fanatic. He is a fit leader of the rebellion, and would be a fit ruler: he deserves the admiration bordering on worship that Winston feels for him.

There is undoubtedly some resemblance between this understanding of the highest human type and the man of wisdom and virtue described in classical philosophy. Both views maintain that man is essentially a rational and social animal, and that the development of these elements produces the most admirable and happiest individual. But the differences between the two views are equally striking. The classics spoke directly and extensively of what they had in mind, delineating the theoretical and practical functions of reason. They subjected the various moral virtues to analysis. They acknowledged the need for controlling instinct and emotion and for habituating the young to such control through a proper moral education, to which they devoted much attention. And they insisted that, since only the wise and virtuous could furnish the best political rule, political rule deteriorated insofar as it came under the influence of the unwise or vicious. But Orwell's upbringing as a modern liberal socialist did not dispose him to such conclusions. He constantly tended to assume that men could live well and happily if only the proper material conditions were provided to them within a democratic framework, where they could act for the common good in a manner fully consistent with the utmost freedom for the individual and his desires. Remove scarcity and poverty and the fundamental human problem was solved: strife and oppression would disappear.

Something like this view, at any rate, pervaded all his earlier writings and would seem to underlie his conception of the perfect human society. Not that this faith was unaccompanied by doubts: as we have seen, Orwell was much more concerned than most of his contemporaries about the ends to be pursued, the standard to be maintained, the limits to be observed in a highly technological socialist society. But he had preserved his faith despite his doubts, and tried to keep both, in spite of their inconsistency.

The Greatest Evil

That Orwell could not finally have held to this simplistic view of the sources of evil and oppression is demonstrable from his treatment of the causes of evil in Oceania. Since O'Brien the Inner Party leader is the prototype of evil, and since the last chapter of the work is mainly devoted to a confrontation of his and Winston's deepest motives, let us turn now to those unforgettable scenes. In them Winston is being forcibly converted to orthodoxy. He thinks of himself as defending the human heritage by upholding both reality's independence of political fiat and the value of loyalty to those we love. But in the end he is vanquished by O'Brien, who literally tears apart his physical and mental being and reconstitutes him as something no longer human. His resolve to preserve the dictates of his intellect perishes first, then his loyalty to Julia, and he finally comes to love Big Brother.

We should begin with the kind of evil done to Winston, for it is clear from the amount of space occupied by these particulars that Orwell intended to impress them upon the reader. First he is subjected to violent beatings, mental humiliation, and nervous exhaustion. Then O'Brien uses an electrical rack, a mind-pulverizer, and Room 101's "worst thing in the world" to demolish his intellectual and moral power completely.[45] O'Brien is a strange mixture of the doctor, teacher, priest, and sadist. He admits to desiring power for its own sake, and making Winston an assenting part of the regime's world is somehow essential to him. But why is power desirable? The rationale runs something like this. The major premise is that every human being is doomed to die, and that death is the greatest of all failures. To overcome death is the most important thing, and this can only be accomplished by merging one's identity with an eternal human collective—i.e., with the Party. But such a collective can be imperishable only if it is all-powerful, only if all other things are at its command. This in turn can only occur if all reality exists within human minds, so that controlling the beliefs of men is in fact to control reality. Now the only way of assuring one's control over the minds of others is by compelling belief in, and obedience to, one's every dictate. Thus, the only way a member of the Party can feel all-powerful and gain testimonial to his own immortality is to engage in acts of compelling belief and obedience: hence his constant need for heretics or victims. But if the actions and beliefs of the victim are simply forced, one cannot have the satisfaction of knowing that one's own judgments are always correct and based on truth, and the possibility that one is not omniscient necessarily draws with it the possibility that one is not omnipotent. What is needed, therefore, is forced but voluntary agreement and obedience on the victim's part, and this, paradoxically, is just what O'Brien seeks. Winston is tortured into changing his mind of his own accord—into overcoming his own willfully evil obstinacy.[46]

It is also in keeping with this rationale that the Inner Party should itself be more capable of Doublethinking than any other group in society, for only in this way can it alter its judgments and dictates while continuing to believe that it never changes its mind and never errs. Its immortality is therefore proved by its omniscience and its maleficent omnipotence. Nothing is independent of its momentary will and judgment, and any rebellious attempt to insist on a reality and a standard beyond its control must be mercilessly stamped out. The very natures of things must be removed, and O'Brien makes it clear to Winston that he is especially intent on destroying all that Winston regards as the best in man:

> Never again will you be capable of ordinary human feeling. Everything will be dead inside you. Never again will you be capable of love, or friendship, or joy of living, or laughter, or curiosity, or courage, or integrity. You will be hollow. We shall squeeze you empty, and then we shall fill you with ourselves.[47]

There will also be "no art, no literature, no science." All the typically human characteristics will be sacrificed to the Party's lust for power, and, contrary to Winston's desperate hope, O'Brien insists that there is neither in life, nor in man, nor in the universe any moral principle or cause which can oppose and defeat the Party.

Let us now compare the assumptions underlying the ways of life of Winston and O'Brien. To begin with, both explicitly agree that God does not exist and that the individual human soul is not immortal. Without this fundamental atheism, the positions taken by each would be unintelligible. For it is fear of his own mortality that drives O'Brien to try to become God: "We are the priests of power. God is power." As part of the Party, he becomes part of the Absolute and places himself beyond the processes of perishing. Winston, however, bases his life on the recognition that he is and must remain a man, limited in power and eventually doomed to die and disappear forever, and when confronted by the claims made by O'Brien for the regime and by the actual power of the regime, he attempts to fall back on some principle that will serve as a source of the strength needed to guard the good for men, the human heritage. But the best he can have recourse to is "the spirit of Man."[48]

It seems, then, that the eternal and the absolute play a vital role in the considerations of both men. Earlier in the novel there are also several instances of Winston's desire to share in the future of Man, or to enjoy an eternally undisturbed state of serene love or thought. And we have already seen that one feature of O'Brien the rebel as the highest human type is his strength and durability: "When you looked at O'Brien's powerful shoulders and his blunt-featured face, so ugly and yet so civilized, it was impossible to believe that he could be defeated." These examples of what Winston desires and admires suggest an agreement with O'Brien (the Party leader) to the effect that the best state of existence would be one in which good activities are carried on by eternal, self-determining beings: only in this way could the good be fully protected. On the other hand, the two men differ profoundly as to what things are good and whether man can become absolute. For O'Brien, one of the natural desires—the desire for self-preservation—is made the dominant motivating force. The fear of death rules all else, and in order for the self to be assured that it need not and cannot perish, the rest of the rationale must follow. Thus, despite what O'Brien says, it is clear that he does not in fact seek power or inflict cruelty for their own sakes: these are only the means of confirming his own indestructibility. But Orwell's point is that to try to make oneself absolute in this sense is not only to guarantee one's failure but also to do the utmost harm to oneself and one's fellows. It is the way of madness, and of the greatest evil.

The case for Winston is very different. His own good is seen to depend on preserving all the parts of his nature—especially his intellect and his concern for others. But preserving his intellect involves acknowledging that there is a reality independent of human desire, will, and even perception. And care for other men involves supplying them with what their nature requires. In both instances Winston is harmonized with other things because he needs their being what they are in themselves if his own nature is to be fulfilled. It would be better if one could live forever, and if the human race were eternal. But these must remain mere wishes: personal immortality is impossible, and even the continuance of the species is something to be striven for but hardly guaranteed. Human perfection requires accepting the fact of death and concentrating on those elements of human nature that are specific to man alone and elevate him above the brutes. Any other course leads to non-humanity and inhumanity.

Winston's Defeat

Convinced though Winston is of his personal mortality, it is nevertheless the overpowering natural urge to keep himself alive and free from pain and terror that eventually makes possible his defeat at the hands of the regime. By lacking the self-control necessary for committing suicide while there was still time (although others had been able to), he gave himself over to tortures which few if any could withstand. O'Brien's aim in these tortures is to destroy Winston's mind, his loyalty, his sense of personal worth, his independence of will—in short, his specifically human nature. But there is a problem in the fact that Winston surrenders his intellect before his feelings. He hears the recording of his own earlier revolutionary oath pledging a willingness to inflict suffering on the innocent for the sake of the revolution; he is shown the wreck of his body; it is demonstrated to him that the Party has complete knowledge of his life. Eventually—in the face of such testimony to the Party's power and his own weakness, and after being tortured by machines—he submits intellectually: the Party is right in its judgments, and he begins to learn Doublethink. But he still loves Julia and hates the Party, and resolves to do so covertly till he is put to death:

> In the old days he had hidden a heretical mind beneath an appearance of conformity. Now he had retreated a step further: in the mind he had surrendered, but he had hoped to keep the inner heart inviolate.[49]

What might account for Orwell's having Winston surrender his reason before his feelings? Rational judgment is as much a natural function of human beings as loving, but it necessarily involves a relation with the thing judged by which its adequacy is measured. In loving, however, there is only an emotion directed toward some object. The emotion is there inside us and cannot, like a judgment, be true or false to its object—which seems to give it a more protected status. In addition, feeling as such may appear to be more deeply rooted in our animal nature than thinking. To stay human, to preserve the human heritage in the long run might therefore mean to hold on to one's human feelings even more than one's thoughts. But Winston is not even permitted to keep his love for Julia or his hatred for the Party. O'Brien forces him to betray Julia by confronting him with what for him is the worst thing in the world: rats.

> "By itself," he [O'Brien] said, "pain is not always enough. There are occasions when a human being will stand out against pain, even to the point of death. But for everyone there is something unendurable—something that cannot be contemplated. Courage and cowardice are not involved. If you are falling from a height it is not cowardly to clutch at a rope. If you have come up from deep water it is not cowardly to fill your lungs with air. It is merely an instinct which cannot be disobeyed. It is the same with the rats. For you, they are unendurable. They are a form of pressure you cannot withstand, even if you wish to. You will do what is required of you."[50]

As predicted, Winston betrays Julia, and she—given the same treatment—betrays him: each wishes the other to be put in his place in Rm. 101:

You think there's no other way of saving yourself and you're quite ready to save yourself that way. You want it to happen to the other person. You don't give a damn what they suffer. All you care about is yourself.[51]

O'Brien himself admits that men differ greatly in the extent to which pain can cause them to betray worthwhile causes. Some, when they can, commit suicide beforehand; some will stand out against certain forms of pain even to death. All, however, can be vanquished by the particular application that their living being finds unendurable: beyond some point, every man will put his own care before his care for others. Clearly O'Brien is in effect forcing his victims to recognize that fundamentally, by nature, they are like himself—i.e., essentially selfish. The destruction of his own being is what he admittedly wants most to avoid, and he can claim that only his own way of life consistently follows the deepest dictates of human nature. Thus ultimate disagreement between Winston and O'Brien is based on an ultimate agreement, to the effect that the proper life for man is the one most in accord with his nature. The ultimate difference is over the interpretation of what human nature requires. But O'Brien has not really proven his case. Apart from the inadequacies of his own attempt to gain actual immortality, all he has shown is that the force of circumstance is sometimes too strong for the unselfishness of all men, and in the process he has in fact demonstrated the enormous possibilities for noble action that human nature allows and encourages in most circumstances.

Nature, it is true, has not provided our natural inclinations with a strength proportionate to their dignity, and it has not even provided us with a steady knowledge of their relative dignity. The human animal is, after all, an animal. But these apparent lacks are the very basis of human nobility, just as they also make possible human vice: if noble action constantly occurred by a kind of natural necessity in the species, would it be noble? Are angels noble? Does not nobility require a struggle of the higher elements against the lower—a struggle pitting insight, reasoning, character, and choice against powerful instincts, emotions, and prejudices? This is why some men will undergo great torment and die for their convictions, or for others, and are admired for it. And even Winston, who lacked the courage to kill himself before being captured by the Thought Police, is not really like O'Brien. He does betray Julia, but he then suffers shame and utter moral collapse because he knows he willed undeserved harm to someone he loved. Winston is defeated, but is it because of a personal defect or because his philosophy is wrong? Having arranged for the confrontation of the two men and their views, Orwell leaves it to the reader to decide between them, but not without suggesting his own solution. He has elaborated the humanist ethic and subjected it to its greatest modern challenge—a challenge deriving ultimately not from material defects in society but from the decay of Christian belief and the attempt to find a political substitute for its promise of personal immortality. But who really wins this struggle? We see that Winston gives in only after his human nature is destroyed by artificial forces that reduce him to an animal. O'Brien really loses because we know his belief in his power over reality is completely insane.

Part Three
From Earthly Paradise to Earthly Hell

Origins of the Regime

So far we have concentrated on Orwell's attempt in *1984* to present a much-needed teaching concerning the goods and evils of human life. But another of his major objectives is to explain the causes of the crisis of liberal civilization in the twentieth century. How has it happened that the time of greatest promise for the Earthly Paradise brings forth perfect despotism instead? In order to convey his answer to this question, Orwell arranges for Winston's reading "The Theory of Oligarchical Collectivism"—a lengthy treatise purportedly written by the underground's leader, Emmanuel Goldstein.

Later in the story, doubt is cast on the truthfulness of this treatise by O'Brien's revelation that it was prepared by the Inner Party itself. But he also informs Winston of its descriptive accuracy, and it coincides so well with what we have already learned about the regime through Winston and Julia that Winston himself fully accepts the parts he reads as the true account of the regime's essential nature. It does, however, delve into matters of which he could have had no firsthand knowledge when it traces the historical background and actual genesis of the regime, and to these points we turn now.

The chronology of events culminating in the rule of Big Brother and the Inner Party can be gathered from remarks in both the treatise and previous parts of the novel. In the middle 1950's a great atomic war breaks out in which "some hundreds of bombs were dropped on industrial centers, chiefly in European Russia, Western Europe and North America." This war leads to civil wars and revolutions, with great ideological battles and purges occurring in the late 1950's and the 1960's. By the next decade, Big Brother and his Party have become the dictators of Oceania, an empire spanning the British Isles and the Western hemisphere and one of three controlling the whole world.

The aim of Oceania's regime, which calls itself Ingsoc or English socialism, is discussed by Goldstein against the background of a general conception of history and of the ideal society:

> Throughout recorded time, and probably since the end of the Neolithic Age, there have been three kinds of people in the world, the High, the Middle, and the Low.[52]

All history has been the history of class struggle, with only the Lows at times really seeking the establishment of a society of equals. But the Lows—the common working people—have never succeeded. Their physical condition may be ameliorated, as in recent centuries especially, but the abolition of class distinctions has never been accomplished. From the slave rebellions of antiquity to the socialism of the nineteenth century, a long chain of thought has upheld "the idea of an earthly paradise in which men should live together in a state of brotherhood, without laws and without brute labor...." In earlier ages, however,

> ...class distinctions had not been only inevitable but desirable. Inequality was the price of civilization. With the development of machine production, however, the case was altered. Even if it was still necessary for human beings to do different kinds of work, it was no longer necessary for them to live at different social or economic levels.[53]

By the early twentieth century,

> ...the vision of a future society unbelievably rich, leisured, orderly, and efficient—a glittering antiseptic world of glass and steel and snow-white concrete—was part of the consciousness of nearly every literate person. Science and technology were developing at a prodigious speed, and it seemed natural to assume they would go on developing.[54]

Yet somehow by the fourth decade of the twentieth century,

> ...all the main currents of political thought were authoritarian. The earthly paradise had been discredited at exactly the moment when it became realizable. Every new political theory, by whatever name it called itself, led back to hierarchy and regimentation.[55]

Thus it is that through the atomic wars of the 1950's, already widely existing totalitarian tendencies are given an opportunity to grow swiftly and win out everywhere, so that by 1984 three super-states basically similar to Oceania rule the earth with every sign of permanence.

Orwell's problem here is to explain how the moment of greatest expectancy for modern liberal socialism could have such an issue. First, as to the social background of Oceania's rulers:

> The new aristocracy was made up for the most part of bureaucrats, scientists, technicians, trade-union organizers, publicity experts, sociologists, teachers, journalists and professional politicians. These people, whose origins lay in the salaried middle class and the upper grades of the working class, had been shaped and brought together by the barren world of monopoly industry and centralized government. As compared with their opposite numbers in past ages, they were less avaricious, less tempted by luxury, hungrier for pure power, and, above all, more conscious of what they were doing and more intent on crushing opposition. This last difference was cardinal. By comparison with that existing today, all the tyrannies of the past were half-hearted and inefficient.[56]

This group is remarkable for the extent to which intellectuals and experts of one sort of another predominate in it, and, as we have seen, the torture scenes involving O'Brien and

Winston are especially intended to elucidate the special nature and source of its power-hunger. In order to establish its own permanent dominion it must eliminate the possible causes of rebellion, including the threat emanating from technological productivity itself. It does so through its scientific knowledge of nature, machines, and men—i.e., through those very sciences and inventions whose progress is the pride of the modern West. At the regime's inception, the technology of mass control was already in an advanced state:

> ...in the past no government had the power to keep its citizens constantly under surveillance. The invention of print, however, made it easier to manipulate the public opinion, and the film and the radio carried the process further. With the development of television, and the technical advance which made it possible to receive and transmit simultaneously on the same instrument, private life came to an end.[57]

Once in power, the regime employs scientific research for only two purposes: "One is how to discover, against his will, what another human being is thinking, and the other is how to kill several hundred people in a few seconds without giving warning beforehand."[58] Finally, the regime has at its command a thorough knowledge of history. It knows why its tyrannical predecessors failed and consciously gears all its practices and institutions—from collectivism and the trappings of socialism to Doublethink—to the prevention of successful opposition.[59] Orwell's view of the overall development of modern Western

civilization seems therefore to be something like this: man
rebels against the restrictions of God and nature and thereby
renders the Earthly Paradise possible but in so doing he creates
individuals far more power-hungry than before, instruments—
both scientific and technological—whereby these individuals
can rule over the majority without their consent, and
situations—such as atomic wars—which give them and their
party machines the opportunity they require. For the sake of
power—ultimately for their own unending self-preservation—
they proceed to distort and destroy human nature itself, so that
the original revolt for human freedom and brotherhood
terminates in unparalleled oppression. The dream of an Earthly
Paradise results in an Earthly Hell.

Prediction or Warning?

For one who never relinquished humanism and democratic
socialism in principle, this is an extraordinary position, and we
must now attempt to determine, first, how seriously Orwell
held it, and second, what his aim was in describing—prior to
its actual occurrence—this evil transformation of modern
civilization. We should begin by discounting the widely-held
view that he adopted *1984*'s pessimism concerning the course
of world events as a device for warning and frightening his
contemporaries rather than as a serious forecast of the probable
or necessary future. And we must do so even in the face of a
post-publication statement by Orwell himself to this effect.
For there is evidence to the contrary within the novel. In order
to alert men to a pressing danger, one does not require (and
should, indeed, eschew) a broad theory linking modern

oligarchical collectivism with the oligarchical nature of all human societies. Furthermore, no clear political alternatives to Oceania are envisaged. Even without atomic war there seems to be no ground for political optimism—certainly none in the direction of the ideal society. Regimentation and collectivization are taken to be the general twentieth-century trend in democracies as well as totalitarian dictatorships. In fact, as we remarked earlier, Orwell shows every sign of having finally adopted James Burnham's theory of history and the general format of his oligarchical predictions for the world.

In various writings between 1940 and 1949, Orwell also leaves little doubt about the likelihood he attached to the coming of atomic war and the spread of totalitarianism. Here are some characteristic passages:

> While I have been writing this essay another European war has broken out. It will either last several years and tear Western civilization to pieces, or it will end inconclusively and prepare the way for yet another war which will do the job once and for all.... Almost certainly we are moving into an age of totalitarian dictatorships—an age in which freedom of thought will be at first a deadly sin and later on a meaningless abstraction.[60] (1940)

> Since about 1930 the world has given no reason for optimism whatever. Nothing is in sight except a welter of lies, hatred, cruelty and ignorance, and beyond our present trouble loom vaster ones which are only now entering into the European consciousness.[61] (1944)

It is too early to say in just what way the Russian regime will destroy itself. If I had to make a prophecy, I should say that a continuation of the Russian policies of the last fifteen years…can only lead to a war conducted with atom bombs, which will make Hitler's invasion look like a tea-party.[62] (1946)

These and kindred questions (about Gandhi's political views) need discussion, and need it urgently, in the few years left to us before somebody presses the button and the rockets begin to fly. It seems doubtful whether civilization can stand another major war, and it is at least thinkable that the way out lies through non-violence.[63] (1949)

These passages assume a certain ability to predict human affairs that Orwell—unlike the orthodox Marxists—did not simply take for granted. Rational action requires one to know the forces and trends at work in the world, even if one is to oppose them. In 1945 Orwell made an analysis of his own earlier predictions in order to grasp the difficulties of prediction in general. He found that wishful thinking—among the intellectuals "nationalistic" thinking of one sort or another—is what vitiates predictions. He notes that:

The most intelligent people seem capable of holding schizophrenic beliefs, of disregarding plain facts, of evading serious questions with debating society repartees, of swallowing baseless rumors and of looking on indifferently while history is falsified.

All these mental vices spring ultimately from the nationalistic habit of mind, which is itself, I suppose, the product of fear and of the ghostly emptiness of machine civilization. But at any rate it is not surprising that in our age the followers of Marx have not been much more successful as prophets than the followers of Nostradamus.[64]

In 1947 Orwell refers to his earlier analysis of predictions in the following manner:

My conclusion was that though one is bound to be wrong in detail, one should be able to foresee broad developments correctly if one excludes wish-thinking and fear-thinking. This involves saying a great deal that is unpopular, and in a world like the present one it involves being almost consistently pessimistic. You were unpopular in 1938, for instance, if you said that war was coming shortly, although the fact had been unmistakable for several years past. You are unpopular now if you say that another war is coming up over the horizon: but that seems to me the balance of the probability, and I shall not be deterred from saying it by the charge that I am "doing the work of fascism."[65]

Such evidence compels the conclusion that throughout the post-war period (up to and including 1949, the year *1984* was published), Orwell regarded a great atomic war as extremely probable, and not far off. In the novel itself an atomic war is

needed but once (it occurs in the mid 1950's) to convince the
various resulting regimes that their own power requires the
suspension of such warfare, but it is needed that once.

Turning now to the consequences of the war, what reason
was there for Orwell to think not only that something like
Ingsoc would prevail in Oceania but that it would have
counterparts in the neo-Bolshevism of Eurasia (mainly Russia
and Northwestern Europe) and the Death Worship or
Obliteration of Self in Eastasia (mainly China and Japan)? By
his own admission in the last quotation above, the details of
the future world-settlement—e.g., the boundaries of the super-
states—would seem to come under the heading of the
unpredictable, and that an Oceania straddling the Atlantic
should constitute one country is even improbable. It is easier
to see that Orwell might have supposed the already existing
power of Russian and Chinese Communism to be superior to
all opposing forces in their respective areas. But to understand
why the war and its aftermath would bring a communist-type
regime into existence in Oceania, we must remember his
estimate of the intellectuals of the West. The time of the
individual heretic—the man of integrity and courage who
speaks his own mind—is fast passing in the twentieth century.
The totalitarian outlook and its reversion to political orthodoxy
is growing, but not because of the public at large, which is "too
sane and too stupid" to acquire this outlook. "The direct,
conscious attack on intellectual decency comes from the
intellectuals themselves."[66]

The social recruitment of Oceania's ruling element is
generally the same as that attributed by Orwell to the English
Russophiles in his essay on Burnham. Such groups, whether

or not they are initially communist or Russophile, exist in all advanced industrial societies and would organize for the seizure of power once atomic war had destroyed the fabric of constitutionalism and liberty. In the ensuing civil wars, the combination of socialistic appeal with the disciplined use of fraud and force might very well guarantee their victory, not only in England but in that stronghold of capitalism—the United States—as well. Thus, through the spreading of communist-type regimes, the liberation of the intellect begun in modern times eventuates in the victory of power-hungry intellect over humane intellect. A communism that unites the language of reason and humanity with the barbaric practices it shares with fascism is the wave of the future. Only it has the knowledge and skill permitting it to function simultaneously as the heir and executioner of modern liberal civilization. Only it, rather than fascism, can be symbolized in O'Brien's unique synthesis of the civilized man of reason and the ruthless fanatic and persecutor. We should also note in this connection that the proles are portrayed as having no need for religion. The horizon within which they live is the ancestral pattern of work and family. Biblical religion, therefore, cannot be regarded as the opiate of the people, who without it are already custom-bound. Its vital function, Orwell implies, was to inspire and restrain the intellectuals and to protect society from the assault of their emancipated ambition. For O'Brien and the Inner Party wish to be divine, and their Outer Party minions are driven by "nationalism" and fear to seek affiliation with the divine. Modern machine civilization leads ultimately, then, to a regime far worse than the Catholic Middle Ages. By its rationalist debunking and spiritual emptiness it prepares the

emergence of self-deified intellectualism operating beyond the
bounds of traditional morality.

Why No Political Alternatives

We must now attempt to understand more thoroughly
Orwell's despair concerning the strength of non-totalitarian
forces throughout the world. Why does *1984* convey a positive
moral but not a positive political message? For Orwell the non-
totalitarian orderings of human society still represented in the
pre-atomic war world are either predominantly agrarian or
industrial, with the latter ranging in degree of state control
from the laissez-faire still strong in America to England's
situation under the Labor Party. As for the agrarian alternative,
we observe that *1984* is entirely lacking in rural characters. It
concentrates on life in London (Airstrip One) and only
mentions the countryside and farmers in the account of
Winston's first rendezvous with Julia. The proles are always city
proles, and no information at all is given concerning the
manner in which the regime controls the rural population.
Since the plot focuses on the revolt of an intellectual of the
Outer Party, it is perhaps plausible that much of the action
should have an urban location. In addition, the city is the area
most subject to control by the regime, whether through
telescreens (for the Outer Party) or mass demonstrations (for
the proles). It reveals most completely the artificial re-
structuring of human life accomplished in Oceania.
Nevertheless, there must be some further reason why the
farmer—his way of life, the devices for controlling his potential
revolt—is not treated somewhere, possibly in Goldstein's

treatise. In earlier writings Orwell deplores the left-wing's heavy discrimination in favor of the city and against the farm people, but in *1984* the scope of his own attention has a similar limit.

We have already seen that Orwell's writings occasionally express a preference for pre-industrial over industrial civilization. These utterances simply constitute a protest against the evils of machine-based society in favor of a more natural life, but they are never elaborated. Something similar happens in *1984*. It is clear from the significance the countryside has for Winston that its natural beauty and freedom must remain vital ingredients of the good life: to be himself, man needs to retain contact with, and imitate, external nature. But the theory of history in Goldstein's treatise depicts primarily agricultural societies as the natural home of inequality and deprivation, though without the cities they sometimes supported, civilization would have been impossible. Without the transformation of these cities into industrial centers, however, there is no material basis for human equality and brotherhood. The ultimate disillusionment for Orwell consists in the realization that the ideal society is also impossible on the basis of industrialization, for there is a direct causal connection between industrialized urban society and Oceania's regime. The city—long the support and hope of Western civilization—becomes its most decadent part and hence the perfect symbol of what Orwell seeks to convey. Nor can the trend it symbolizes be reversed, as the treatise itself makes clear:

> To return to the agricultural past, as some thinkers about the beginning of the twentieth century

dreamed of doing, was not a practicable solution. It conflicted with the tendency toward mechanization which had become quasi-instinctive throughout almost the whole world, and moreover, any country which remained industrially backward was helpless in a military sense and was bound to be dominated, directly or indirectly, by its more advanced rivals.[67]

Unfortunately, Orwell permits the impracticability of the pre-industrial alternative to deter him from assessing its overall merit in theory, in the direction of classical political philosophy. But if Oceania represents the probable coming of the worst of all societies, one cannot escape the conclusion that the turn toward industrialization and a society based on science and technology was the greatest error man could make. Orwell probably felt this conclusion, but he could not bring himself to express it directly, or to examine its full consequences.

As for alternatives among industrialized societies, Orwell never doubted that liberal capitalistic democracy is greatly superior to both Nazi and Communist totalitarianism, and over many years he expended no little energy attempting to demonstrate as much to fellow left-wingers. Its rule of law, democracy, civil liberties, improved standard of living, moral decency were all in its favor, and in *1984* explicit tribute is paid to the accomplishments of the French, English, and American revolutions and especially to their ideals, culminating in the appendix's quotation from the Declaration of Independence. Nevertheless, Orwell was convinced that capitalism could not last, even without atomic wars. In its final stage capitalism signifies "a barren world of monopoly industry and centralized government." It cannot solve the problem of overproduction and under-consumption with liberal methods. It is necessarily depression-ridden, and in revolutionary times will not be able to withstand the onslaught of the combination of power-hungry experts and dissatisfied public.

The quasi-Marxist belief that capitalist democracy is doomed and must either give way to democratic socialism or some species of totalitarianism was formed much earlier by Orwell and later amended only to exclude the democratic socialist alternative. In the essay on Burnham, he takes issue with Burnham and affirms the vigor of free capitalism in the United States, adding, however, that "even in the United States the all-prevailing faith in laissez-faire may not survive the next great economic crisis." But concerning the world-trend he believes Burnham's thesis to have considerable validity:

> For quite fifty years past the general drift has almost certainly been toward oligarchy. The ever-increasing concentration of industrial and financial power; the diminishing importance of the individual capitalist or shareholder, and the growth of the new "managerial" class of scientists, technicians and bureaucrats; the weakness of the proletariat against the centralized state; the increasing helplessness of small countries against big ones; the decay of representative institutions and the appearance of one-party regimes based on police terrorism, faked plebiscites, etc.; all these things seem to point in the same direction.[68]

Nor was Orwell more optimistic concerning democratic socialist prospects. During the post-war years he thought less and less of the desirability of revolution, and in England, where the Labor Party was voted into office, no fundamental transformation of the social structure was undertaken. Moreover, the English Russophile left-wingers who might be expected to undertake such a transformation would in reality seek something very different from true socialism.

For reasons of this kind Orwell seems seriously to have concluded that the future lay with such regimes as those pictured in his novel. Under the pressure of forces born of secular machine civilization itself, today's ordinary man and decent intellectual are both probably doomed to servitude in the worst of possible societies that is the last stage of modernity. In *1984* Orwell tries to imagine the nature of this last stage, using currently existing trends to develop its principles in their perfection. In some such form, Oceania is on its way.

Motives for Writing *1984*

This is the evidence that can be given to show how seriously Orwell meant Oceania as a forecast, and what he was least guilty of was the partisan favoring of one's own group that he believed characteristic of the intellectuals of his time. But in 1948—the same year that he spoke about the difficulties of prediction and the need to be pessimistic in the post-war period—he also called himself a "political" writer, who ever since 1936 had been using his pen to advance the cause of democratic socialism and oppose totalitarianism, who always started from a sense of injustice and was animated by "...a desire to push the world in a certain direction, to alter other people's idea of the kind of society that they should strive after." Since he alludes in this same place to a political novel he intends to write, incorporating his greatest effort to fuse art and politics, and since he probably had in mind what was to become *1984*, we must work on the assumption that there too his purpose was "political." Now to have such a purpose is to think that men can be influenced by what one writes and therefore that the course of events can in some degree be altered by literary action. It is to presume that the future is not wholly determined independently of such action. How, then, was Orwell attempting to influence human history? What were his major objectives in writing and publishing *1984*?

In answering this question we must constantly have recourse to Orwell's earlier writings, and of these his longest essay—the one on Dickens—offers the most assistance. Dickens, as Orwell interprets him, "was certainly a subversive writer, a radical, one might truthfully say, a rebel." But he did not encourage revolutionary change at the political and social level, and in fact had no idea of what a better political and social system would be. His radicalism was moral: "His whole 'message' is one that at first glance looks like an enormous platitude: If men would behave decently the world would be decent." In addition, he had no perception of an historic necessity independent of the wills of men. He was certainly not a Karl Marx. In fact, Orwell criticizes Dickens for not having enough Marx in him. He did not see that private property is an obstacle, nor that social progress keeps occurring, nor that political government is essential, nor that social equality is desirable; he lacked interest in work, machinery, and technical progress. "He has no constructive suggestions, not even a clear grasp of the nature of the society he is attacking, only an emotional perception that something is wrong." But Dickens is still a real revolutionary. He hates tyranny: "As a matter of course he is on the side of the underdog, always and everywhere." He worries about justice and about the moral quality of human life. He is "…a free intelligence, a type hated with equal hatred by all the smelly little orthodoxies which are now contending for our souls."[69] What an unforgettable phrase!

The following year Orwell learned of an attitude diametrically opposed to both the moral protest of Dickens and the social protest of Marx. His deeply pessimistic essay on Henry Miller speaks of political quietism as the final literary mood of doomed liberalism:

> It seems likely, therefore, that in the remaining years of free speech any novel worth reading will follow more or less along the lines that Miller has followed—I do not mean in technique or subject matter, but in implied outlook. The passive attitude will come back, and it will be more consciously passive than before. Progress and reaction have both turned out to be swindles. Seemingly there is nothing left but quietism—robbing reality of its terrors by simply submitting to it. Get inside the whale—or rather, admit you are inside of the whale (for you are, of course). Give yourself over to the world-process, stop fighting against it or pretending

that you control it; simply accept it, endure it, record it. That seems to be the formula that any sensitive novelist is now likely to adopt. A novel on more positive, "constructive" lines, and not emotionally spurious, is at present very difficult to imagine.[70]

A few years later two additional alternatives presented themselves to Orwell. One was the Machiavellianism he saw in James Burnham, which encouraged acting in the world not against injustice and the trends but with them. The other was Arthur Koestler's withdrawal from political action after he had lost hope for revolutionary socialism, attempting, as Orwell put it, to stay in an oasis "within which you and your friends can remain sane"—in short, the attitude of Marxism in despair.

1984 can best be interpreted as Orwell's final response to these various possibilities. It is the work of a disappointed political revolutionary for whom moral rather than political solutions have become supremely important. It accepts Burnham's understanding of history rather than Marx's, but not his Machiavellianism; it accepts Koestler's pessimism about revolution but not his withdrawal; it rejects Miller's quietism. Its real essence is Dickens, but a Dickens equipped with political interest and knowledge and concerned about the moral destiny of modern man. In the face of, and through, extreme political pessimism it attempts to show modern men their dilemma and to teach them to be human in a godless universe.

Who are the addressees of *1984*? Who are the men who could understand its political analyses and ethical message? Certainly not the proles, and probably not those like O'Brien who are consciously bent on establishing their own tyrannical rule. It is to the potential Outer Party—to the great variety of educated intellectuals and experts who will in all likelihood constitute the major human instruments and objects of the new tyranny—that Orwell speaks. But we have no way of knowing either the extent to which he thought he might be able to strengthen their support of liberal humanism, or the influence this might have in averting the victory of totalitarianism. He undoubtedly saw that the odds were against him. In *The Road to Wigan Pier* he acknowledges how widespread among left-wingers are the traits that would corrupt any socialist revolution. In *Animal Farm* not a single revolutionary intellectual is favorably portrayed. And *1984* itself gives the strong impression that such types as Winston are rare in the Outer Party and would be so even without the influence of the Thought Police.

The first need of the intellectuals was for more accurate information about the workings of communist-type totalitarian regimes. In this way the better ones might be jarred out of their optimistic complacency concerning the threat of such regimes, and the others might lose their sympathy after contemplating the horrors to which they would be subject as members of the Outer Party. And it would serve both purposes if Orwell, like Dickens, could supply his audience with "parlor words" (such as "Big Brother," "Doublethink," "Thought Police") that would make it difficult for them to forget his message. But intellectuals—especially those nourished on Marx—also need to be supplied with a full account of the reasons underlying the downward turn of modern civilization. Above all, they must be brought to comprehend the meaning and necessity of the humanist ethic. For this purpose, Orwell wanted to write a political tragedy in which his protagonist would be equipped with a moral code enabling him to withstand greater tortures than those under which the demoralized Rubashov in Koestler's *Darkness At Noon* surrendered.[71] Like Winston Churchill, and as we can imagine Orwell himself, the intellectuals must be prepared to fight totalitarianism to the death even if they cannot win. The odds, in fact, are against their winning, but only by dedicating themselves to the spirit of Man can there be dignity in either defeat or victory.

In *1984* Orwell produced a kind of literary work which in 1940 was unimaginable even to himself. It does not adopt Miller's apolitical quietism, yet neither is it politically "positive" or "constructive." It attempts to equip men with the moral foundation for whatever political action can achieve and for passing on the human heritage from hand to hand or even mouth to mouth should the threatening blackness engulf them. It speaks for the future nameless millions who might find themselves living under conditions which made it impossible for them to speak for themselves. This was what Orwell's literary art sought to achieve, and this was the closest he could come to acting the part of the Christian God, who knew and cared for all His children. No better account has been given of how the quest for earthly paradise led to earthly hell. It remains the great alarm bell it was meant to be, an unparalleled portrayal of totalitarianism, a classic of Western self-examination, and a drama forcing us to confront the realities of modern life. What more can a political writer do? And has our response been adequate to the challenge?

Notes

For ease of reference, instead of using Orwell's three original collections of essays (*Dickens, Dali and Others, Shooting An Elephant,* and *Such, Such Were the Joys*), I have had recourse to *The Collected Essays, Journalism and Letters of George Orwell* (Harcourt, Brace, New York 1968), edited by Sonia Orwell and Ian Angus in four volumes. The notes supply the volume, page number and source. References to Orwell's books will be *Road* for *The Road To Wigan Pier* (Berkley Publishing Corporation, New York, 2963) and *Coming* for *Coming Up For Air* (Harcourt, Brace, New York, 1939), followed by the page number. For *1984* the Signet Giant edition (1950) is used.

1. IV, 298 *Lear, Tolstoy and the Fool.*
2. IV, 299, ibid.
3. IV, 267 *Reflections on Gandhi.*
4. IV, 219 Politics vs. Literature: An Examination of *Gulliver's Travels.*
5. *Road,* 169.
6. Ibid., 174.
7. II, 265 *Looking Back on the Spanish Civil War.* The preceding quotation is from *Road,* 85.
8. III, 103 *Tribune,* March 3, 1944.
9. IV, 80–81 Tribune January 11, 1946.
10. *Coming,* 192–4.
11. IV, 144 *Thoughts on the Common Toad.*
12. III, 237 *Charles Dickens.*

13. II, 68 The *Lion and the Unicorn.*
14. II, 141 *Charles Dickens.*
15. Ibid., 144.
16. III, 362–363 *Notes on Nationalism.*
17. II, 258 *Looking Back on the Spanish Civil War.*
18. II, 73–75 The *Lion and the Unicorn*; III, 369 *Notes on Nationalism*; I, 515 *Inside the Whale.*
19. III, 380 *Notes on Nationalism*; I, 457–8 *Charles Dickens.*
20. *Road,* 179; IV, 441 *Writers and Leviathan*; II, 258, 266 *Looking Back on the Spanish Civil War*; I, 525–6 *Inside the Whale*; II, 142 *Wells, Hitler and the World State.*
21. I, 525 *Inside the Whale.*
22. III, 240 *Arthur Koestler.*
23. Ibid., 244.
24. Ibid.
25. I, 525 *Inside the Whale.*
26. I, 460 *Charles Dickens.*
27. IV, 408–9 *Writers and Leviathan.*
28. IV, 72 *Tribune,* January 4, 1946.
29. IV, 160–81 *James Burnham and the Managerial Revolution.*
30. *1984,* 16.
31. Ibid., 58.
32. Ibid., 59.
33. Ibid., 75.
34. Ibid., 95.
35. Ibid., 25–6.
36. Ibid., 122–6.
37. Ibid., 126.
38. Ibid., 63.
39. Ibid., 90–7.
40. Ibid., 108, 168.
41. Ibid., 14, 16.
42. Ibid., 114.
43. Ibid., 11, 12, 128–36, 192.
44. Ibid., 56, 66–7; 119, 153; 152, 133, 167–8.

45. Ibid., 186, 215.
46. Ibid., 201; 189, 204, 207.
47. Ibid., 195.
48. Ibid., 205.
49. Ibid., 213.
50. Ibid., 216.
51. Ibid., 222.
52. Ibid., 153.
53. Ibid., 155.
54. Ibid., 143.
55. Ibid., 155.
56. Ibid., 156.
57. Ibid., 156.
58. Ibid., 147.
59. Ibid., 156.
60. I, 525 *Inside the Whale.*
61. III, 243 *Arthur Koestler.*
62. IV, 180 *James Burnham and the Managerial Revolution.*
63. IV, 469 *Reflections on Gandhi.*
64. *Partisan Review,* Winter, 1945, 77–82.
65. *Tribune,* February 7, 1947, 14. See also *III, 364 Notes on Nationalism; Partisan Review,* Summer, 1946, 323.
66. IV, *70 The Prevention of Literature.*
67. *1984,* 144.
68. IV, 176 *James Burnham and the Managerial Revolution.*
69. I, 460, 413 ff. *Charles Dickens.*
70. I, 526 *Inside the Whale.*
71. III, 2 238–49 *Arthur Koestler.*

Index